Horse Lovers

Unpacking the Female Fascination

By Karin Winegar

HORSE FEED PRESS

Horse Lovers: Unpacking the Female Fascination

Author: Karin Winegar
www.karinwinegar.com

Third printing, 2026

Art direction and design by Joan Nygren

Cover Photo by Sally Shepard, © 2025
Karin Winegar with Monty

ISBN: 978-0-578-12523-7
Library of Congress Control Number: 2024920159
Printed in U.S.A.

HORSE FEED PRESS

Publisher: Horse Feed Press
www.horsefeedpress.com

Praise for

Horse Lovers: Unpacking the Female Fascination

"Man's relationship with the horse goes back to prehistory, yet it's our distaff side that seems to become most emotionally captivated by this magnificent quadruped. For more than 30 years, Karin Winegar has written for some of this country's most prestigious news publications and authored six other highly readable books, but through those years she has been mentally probing the elements of this powerful female fascination for this very book, *Horse Lovers.* In its fast-flowing pages, she melds those contemplations with an exciting variety of her equine expeditions around the globe. *Horse Lovers* is a captivating love story of introspection and adventure."

-Norman Fine
Creator and former editor of *Covertside* magazine
and author of award-winning *Blind Bombing: How Microwave Radar Brought the Allies to D-Day and Victory in WWII*

"Horses have changed human history. Since their domestication approximately 4000 years ago, horses have given us strength, speed and power far beyond our physical abilities. Horses have carried soldiers into battle, helped farmers plow their fields, and took countless travelers to their destinations. Until the industrial revolution, horses were the irreplaceable means of transportation and source of energy for human civilizations. They built and sustained nations and empires. Indeed, the ability to domesticate horses may have been key to the development of Asian and European civilizations.

Yet, the true nature of horses is made not for kings, emperors and soldiers, but for women. As social prey animals, they respond to kindness and love much more intensely than to threats and intimidation. A true horseperson has equal measures of courage and empathy, bravery and love. Those are qualities women excel in, and that's why the bond between women and horses is a natural wonder, a deep conversation between creatures of different species that can truly communicate as one.

Horses and horsewomen changed my life. I was raised by my grandmother, a horsewoman born in the19th century, who shared with me her superpowers: grace under fire, self-control, compassion and life-long love of horses. Decades later, I married the love of my life, a brave, loving horsewoman with the very same qualities my grandmother taught me to appreciate. Pictures of the horses my grandmother rode as a girl in the 1890s hang in our living room. My wife and I have built two barns together, rescued many "difficult" horses that have given us much more than we have given them, and introduced many girls to the magnificent animals nature made just for them.

Horsewomen and the magnificent animals they love have much to teach us all about empathy and courage, if we're willing to learn.

This wonderful volume by Karin Winegar opens a window into the unique relationship between two of the most amazing products of evolution: women and horses. I hope you enjoy it as much as I did."

-Lucio Miele, MD, PhD
Horseman, physician and scientist

"What IS it about women and horses, anyhow? What makes us horsey girls love them as our earliest memory in life? What is the obsession? The passion? The connection?

Karin Winegar's fabulous new book, *Horse Lovers*, posits that ageless question at every page turn, and with each turning, we discover a new angle on the elusive and countless possibilities. She shares with us her wonderful collection of horsewomen friends whose lives have been forever changed, defined and enriched by equine partners. Prepare for the most beautifully descriptive armchair travel from a hunt field in Virginia, a wild ride with women way out West, a drive round a Florida estate with one of the world's best coaching women, a tag-along with a rider who twice did the grueling Mongol Derby, or Riding the Marches in the gorgeous Scottish Borders. To each woman in her travels with horses she asks: why do women who love horses seem to do so from the very first breath we inhale?

Karin writes with passion, intelligence, wit, beauty, wisdom and a deep, lifelong love of horses (dogs, wolves and wildlife). Horse Lovers is a book that had me in tears, cheering for the underdogs and the forgotten horses, or breathless in her descriptions of elite equines. It had me shouting affirmations aloud. It will speak to your lifelong horse loving heart and soul."

-Lynne Warfel, national host and producer
American Public Media's *Classical 24*
American Public Media's *Saturday Cinema*

"I loved your book. Wonderful read!"

-Ron Danta, horse trainer, judge,
A-show champion competitor,
Chronicle of the Horse Horseman of the Year 2013
and co-founder of Danny & Ron's Rescue

"If you appreciate writing as a craft. If you've felt lured by horses. Or if you like a deep dive into the whys. For those reasons and more, you may find yourself, as I did, savoring every word and image in Karin Winegar's latest book, *Horse Lovers.* Karin came into this world with a love and longing for horses. It seems those feelings predated speech and an ability to walk. This book explores our human (pervasively female) fascination with horses.

A terrific read. Sumptuous writing. Vivid storytelling. And journalistic scrutiny. Loved it!"

-James Klund
Farrier

"After reading *Horse Lovers: Unpacking the Female Fascination*, I gave it to all my horse enthusiast friends as a must read! In this beautifully written book, Karin Winegar explores the magnetism, devotion and deep connection so many girls and women feel for horses. As someone who was smitten from the first time I sat on a horse, I found kindred spirits in chapter after chapter. An accomplished journalist, Karin Winegar's interviews with horsewomen across different professions yield compelling themes but my favorite segments are her vivid, poignant, and often laugh out loud descriptions of her experiences horseback from riding saucy ponies in childhood to adventures joining the hunt in Virginia, galloping on the beach in Scotland and so much more. A relatable and terrific read."

-Liv Hustvedt
Founder of Yonder Horse

"I was introduced to riding as a kid and didn't fall in love - but did fall in love with this book and immediately ordered a gift for a friend. Honestly, it made me want to go snuggle up with a soft horse face -- and engage in the pas de deux that is riding. Winegar is a gifted writer, deftly weaving personal stories with interviews to explore her central question: Why do women love horses? Power; freedom from feminine trappings of attire and decorum; bonding with a sweet, gentle, huge animal... everything gets considered with no one answer selected. If you love horses, or want to, or love women who do... highly recommended."

-Mariah Burton Nelson,
Former Stanford and pro basketball player,
Award-winning author of *The Stronger Women Get, The More Men Love Football,*
Creator of the Strong Women column on Substack

For all the horsegirls and for
the horse-loving girl in every woman
whether or not she has a horse.

Also for Laurie, Maren, Allie, and
an earth angel named Marianne Doar.

Also by Karin Winegar

Fire and Spice: The Cuisine of Sri Lanka

SAVED: Rescued Animals and the Lives They Transform

Never Stop Dreaming: The Gus Schickedanz Story

High Expectations: The Doug Leatherdale Story

Lost Man Found: Crime, Punishment and Growing a Soul

Nick Legeros: Sculpting a Life

"If we can crystallize the thing going on here, we must be getting into the very nature of femininity. Something in females, something about the essence of femininity is answering and interacting strongly with a horse."

~ **Dr. Elizabeth Lawrence,**
DVM and cultural anthropologist

Introduction

"Those who love horses are impelled by an ever-receding vision, some enchanted transformation through which the horse and the rider become a third, much greater thing."
~Tom McGuane, *Some Horses*

What is it in our brain—mostly female brains—that fires up in some of us in the presence of horses?

If you have chosen to read this, you are almost certainly one of us or want to understand one of us.

There is a reason, or maybe a set of common symptoms, traits, or pre-disposing conditions that define a horse lover, and I am searching for those. I am, I have come to realize, looking not only for the nature of this love but also for the nature of the women who are gripped by it. We are called horse crazy, and there is no treatment for it.

For more than a quarter century, I have traveled farms and stables, horse shows, saddle shops, county and state fairs, equine expositions, and racetracks throughout the United States, Canada, the United Kingdom, and New Zealand, probing into this passion, asking questions about this equine-centered life so many of us share.

Patterns point to how we are similar, why we are seemingly born this way, how the choices we make to be with these powerful animals reflect a certain appetite, spiritually, physically, and mentally.

I want to know what it is, what it isn't, introduce some people and share some of my adventures probing into this joyous, incurable passion.

When we are horse lovers, we enter a world of dangerous liaisons: riding accidents are more common than accidents in skiing, motorcycling, and football and they are more serious (largely head and neck injuries). Riding is the leading cause of traumatic brain injuries (TBIs). To be fair, the fact that many of us refuse to wear helmets factors heavily there. For those of us who love horses truly, madly, deeply, however, those are natural occurrences. They are seldom, if ever, deterrents. We are even a little proud of the price we pay for joy and freedom and a friendship like no other.

In fact, ask any emergency room staff about horsegirls, horsewomen, and horsemen, and they will tell you the first question we pose when we are trundled in is always, "How soon will I be able to ride?" If we are conscious, it is usually preceded by, "Don't cut my boots off, please!"

Is this behavior not a sign of addiction, compulsion, magical thinking? Just what is it?

In general, horses and ponies these days are much better trained than they were when I was given a grade (unregistered) black and white pony and told to "be home for dinner." Molly kicked me twice in the first few minutes as I attempted to jump on her bare back. I wept a bit, mopped my tears on my sweatshirt sleeve and finally clawed myself on. We went off across the fields and into a kind of bliss that perhaps nothing else can provide.

That world of no helmets, often no saddle, no horsemanship instructors, a complete absence of parents helicoptering around the periphery while a child is schooled on a saintly oldster horse is increasingly rare. It was glorious in the ways that freedom spiked with a dash of danger can be. Most of us survived.

Whatever else we were, we were, at the core, horsegirls, one word, two beings welded by sweat and will, love offerings of apples, carrots, and sugar cubes, infinite interest, and occasional pain into one wild, fiercely free thing.

The old barn where I boarded Molly in winter was filled with such girls—lean, manure-shoveling, barrel-racing, log-jumping, tough, gritty girls: Polly, Jan, Cyndy, Becky, Julie, and Jackie. There were only two adults around, men who had grown up farming with horses and now, out of nostalgia, kept a couple for weekend rides.

It was otherwise ours, this entirely all-girl world.

In this converted red dairy barn at the top of a hill, we nailed Christmas stockings on stall doors, pinned horse drawings and show ribbons over the grain bins. We cuddled kittens born in the mangers, hurled curry combs at rats skittering in the rafters, and played Tarzan on the thick cables dangling from blocks in the hayloft.

In summer, we swam our ponies and horses in the nearby lake and dared each other to plunge over the edge and down the crumbling slopes of the local sand pit.

We went to our horses in the mornings, ate peanut butter and jelly sandwiches while lying on their backs, and didn't go home until suppertime. In winter, we fashioned harnesses out of baling twine, cattle ropes and scrap leather and towed each other on sleds and toboggans at perilous hoof level around the snowy barnyard and over the cornfield stubble.

What was the sensation I felt most often then? Aliveness.

Let me recall it for you.

I am riding Molly bareback in the summer heat thick with the aroma of newly cut alfalfa in the fields. I am small enough that her mane whips my face, her choppy pony trot and canter bounce me a bit loose on her silky back. In the warmth of oaks and acorn-infused soil along the banks of the lake, we go into the chattering of robins, the scolding of squirrels, the breeze over limestone gravel. The hollow pounding of her pink hooves—*boom-boom boom-boom boom-boom*—sounds on the wooden bridge where creosote-rich emanations from pilings in the water below are joined by notes of dead carp and rise up again in the perfume of water lilies clustered in the curve of the bank.

To say troubles drop away when we ride is true, but not complete, and not the point. It is what rushes in. It is back to the old gods of the amygdala and raw sensation: fear, desire, triumph, desperation at times, and joy and such joy. That's where being with horses propels me. It's where girls and women find themselves in ever greater numbers and in rising and dramatic disproportion to boys and men.

According to the American Horse Council, some 38 million American households contain a horse enthusiast: of them, 1.3% own a horse, 16% participate but don't own, and 13.2% spectate but don't own or participate. I call them "the yearners" and I hope that someday their yearnings are fulfilled. The median age of an owner is 38 years old; the median age of a participant is 22. Females constitute anywhere from 70 to 85 percent of those 38 million, depending on the source.

Those are the numbers. What is the nature of that relationship, that craving?

At car speed, we may perceive more, but we sense less. We pass through the world but are not of it. On horseback, at the tempo of about six miles an hour, we experience life in a primal way. To ride is to be most perfectly alive, responsible only to stay on and be aware of nothing but ourself and our horse.

It's not that we don't know we are hooked: sometimes I introduce myself to other horse lovers as, "Hi, my name is Karin and I am a horseaholic. It's been 38 hours since I was last in the barn," or something like that. I am not in recovery from this compulsion, however, and indications are that none of us ever will be.

In this book, I look for the words to tell you that riding is something like dance, only with the threat—muted, but occasionally firing upward through your nerves—of harm. Then, subsiding again in roundness, balance, steady breathing, the horse's breath, our sweat, our effort and perhaps something more intangible, intertwined.

I strain for descriptions, something accurate, even just adequate, of what it is to feel, touch, watch, to ride a horse.

I look outward and investigate why we are who we are. I also look inward, at my own family heritage and growing up, for I am after all, an incurable, crazed, bred-in-the-bone horsegirl.

Contents

Preface XIII

Chapter One **Talking Horses** 1

Chapter Two **So Many Horse Books** 7

Chapter Three **Binding Sweethearts** 15

Chapter Four **The 1200-Pound Muscle** 21

Chapter Five **Secret Horses** 29

Chapter Six **Following a Cloud** 35

Chapter Seven **All the Fun of War** 41

Chapter Eight **Horsegirl Psyche** 49

Chapter Nine **Heart Horse** 53

Chapter Ten **Western Challenge** 59

Chapter Eleven **Lady Drivers** 71

Chapter Twelve **Horsegirls Go to the Movies** 79

Chapter Thirteen **Horse Worship** 85

Chapter Fourteen **Genes, Gender, and Other Beings** 91

Chapter Fifteen **The Curse of a Tender Heart** 101

Chapter Sixteen **Galloping Scotland** 113

Chapter Seventeen **Mongol Derby** 121

Chapter Eighteen **Sightings** 131

Chapter Nineteen **Wild at Heart** 137

Chapter Twenty **Horses on the Brain** 141

Afterword **Gone Riding** 149

Acknowledgments 157

Index 159

About the Author 167

Preface

I grew up in a small Minnesota farm town on the Iowa border, the oldest of three contentious, athletic girls, daughters of a petite beauty who was herself athletic and contentious. Mom was the most stylishly dressed woman in town—vivacious, nocturnal and oddly mated to a handsome, quiet, pipe-smoking man who loved trout fishing at dawn and gardening after work.

At nine, after years of begging—and a Christmas where I had been crushed to find a blue Schwinn in the garage instead of a pony—I was ecstatic when Dad bought me Molly, a chubby Welsh-Shetland mare.

By junior high school, my heels hung past her knees when I rode her, and with two younger sisters, Gayle and Jill, expecting to inherit her, I needed—needed! "Dad, really, I do!"—a horse.

So there was Sugar, a cranky, big-boned part-Arabian sorrel mare who once at feeding time kicked me unconscious into the dirt, leaving two purple hoof marks on my narrow chest.

Kicks were not enough to scare the horse craziness out of me. Molly had cow-kicked me (a stealthy sidewise move) frequently as I bounced up and down in my sneakers, trying to summon the momentum to fling myself onto her bare back. Twice, my friend Jan's palomino mare Bunny double-barreled me into the gutter as I passed her in the barn. Nor were falls going to stop me: more than once, while Molly and I were tearing across the icy barnyard in the winter or traversing a slope of the pasture, she slipped and fell on my leg, ripping ligaments and leaving me howling in pain.

Most of the girls I rode with got kicked, bitten, run away with and bucked off; it was routine, and we didn't usually tell our parents.

At twelve or so, I sent away for a pamphlet on horse training from an advertisement in the back of *Western Horseman* magazine. Professor Jesse Berry's trick training booklet featured something called a war bridle, which seemed a lot like things I had rigged out of baling twine for my pony. Riding bareback, two slashes of Helena Rubenstein's Tangee lipstick on my cheeks, I pretended to be a Comanche.

Soon the herd was up to three: Molly produced a silver-gray half-Shetland filly named Filly because we liked the word and couldn't think of another name. For this little herd, Dad rented a small summer pasture a mile away from home. I could bike there in ten minutes or so, and I did this every day.

In late May, amid wild plum trees and old oaks, Sugar gave birth to a leggy sorrel colt with a white blaze. I was the first to touch him, stroking his little bulbous forehead and the fair baby whiskers that curled around his muzzle.

That month, I had been immersed in reading the first truly dark book of my life, Mark Twain's *Letters from the Earth*, and named the colt Gabriael after the ironic angel, throwing in an extra vowel because I thought it sounded more Arabic.

His sire, Gabbar, lived in the next county. A small, exquisite white stallion of Egyptian and Polish Arabian blood who carried himself like a lion, Gabbar was, and I knew Gabe would be, everything I thought I was not. I was shy, bookish and easily stampeded into the woods, the fields or the hayloft of the barn.

The year Gabe was born, I was thirteen, a skinny girl with dishwater blond hair, a mouthful of metal braces, and legs so thin that I used rubber bands under my knee socks and still couldn't keep them up. I loped alone down the corridors of my junior high school, whistling, hitching up my socks every dozen steps, and thinking more about getting to the barn or pasture as fast as possible after school than about my biology assignment. I was going to be a veterinarian, of course, so I could spend all my time with horses, a career with horses being the logical extension of seeing everything through horse-colored glasses.

The barn, the pasture and Gabe were home. When anyone asked, "Where's Karin?" the answer was, "At the horse," as if Gabe were a Platonic form, the embodiment of all horses everywhere. My sisters and mother still describe me a half-century later as "going to the horse" or "out at the horse."

Gabe bloomed from chestnut to steel gray to rose gray. When I was not grooming him or walking him on a lead rope for miles around the neighborhood, I spent my time designing stables on graph paper or filling out wishful order forms for horse gear from Miller Harness Company in Manhattan. I tied strings to the back of my desk chair to practice holding the four reins of a full bridle. I pried the black and blue labels off Kentucky Club Tobacco tins to submit them with entry forms in Name the Colt contests. What would I do if I won that Thoroughbred colt? I had no idea. I just wanted more horses around me.

A life saturated with a love of horses was unfurling.

CHAPTER 1

Talking Horses

"I have always thought that the highest calling of a horse is to make a young girl happy, and all girls, including mature women, are young at heart. They never forget the happiness and sadness, the friendship and emotional connection with a horse they have as a young woman."

~ Philip Odden

Wisconsin breeder and trainer of champion Norwegian Fjord horses

On this early spring evening at a banquet in Caerphilly Castle in Wales, Lord Gordon Parry of Neyland, Chairman of the Wales Tourist Board, steered Prince Charles from visitor to visitor. I was there through a Minnesota friend connected to Lord Parry by a society of Welsh male choirs. As he and Prince Charles approached, I saw him lean toward and presumably brief the Prince before introducing me as an American journalist.

"Hello," I said to Prince Charles, grasping his offered hand. "Whatever happened to your eyes?"

I could get away with this impudence because, at the time, I was young, blond, and swathed tightly from shoulder to toe in black velvet set off with an opera-length string of (fake) pearls. As an American, I was unaware of diplomatic protocol, which dictates that when meeting royals, one must not speak until spoken to. (In my defense, nobody told me this until years later.)

Prince Charles, in black tie below visibly bruised eyes, murmured to me.

"Hello, Miss Winegar, I am pleased to meet you," he began. "How are you enjoying this visit to Wales? I understand you are a journalist?"

"Yes, but don't worry, I am not working today, just savoring this spring trip," I answered. And then I blurted inappropriately at the future (and now) King of England.

I had tottered over the castle cobblestones, through the torchlit keep and into the banquet room on black pumps with four-inch heels newly purchased from Harrod's in London. So I stood straight and immobile thanks to my ridiculous shoes.

No, I was not working, but in direct, reporter-like fashion, I asked the question about his eyes.

"It was a riding accident," said the prince, smiling, and not outwardly the least perturbed. He is, for the record, more attractive than his photos and exuded a kind of genteel attentiveness. Nearby, Diana, Princess of Wales, glided around the same banquet hall, every bit as tall, glamorous, and palely lovely as her photos, moving as if her shoes were not the least bit painful.

Theirs was a mixed marriage, I knew: Diana did not ride, or at least she had not learned when they first met. I do ride and am, in the way of many horsewomen, British, American, or otherwise, obsessed with it.

"What kind of horse were you on?" I asked him. (Wrong again, I now suppose. No questions to royals. Egad.)

"It was a Thoroughbred," he replied.

"You should have been on an Arabian," I said, saucily and utterly wrong-headedly.

At the time, I knew nothing about polo or the fitness it takes to play the game. I was ignorant of the huge blackthorn hedges that riders in British hunts face at speed or the nerve it takes to clear stone walls and do so hour after hour. Or how to survive these sports season after season as Charles had done since childhood.

My interest in everything equine has no boundaries—that's my explanation and occasional excuse. It is not deterred by rank, age or nationality. And while it provides a common and (usually) welcome topic, I wonder if it is a bit of a pathology or a reliable way of overcoming social anxiety as much as it is a truly international language.

One midwinter decades after the Caerphilly Castle incident, I was shopping in my food co-op, and there in the produce section stood three young

Amish men, replete with straw hats, dark blue suits and cascading beards. I groped for a reason to talk with them and found it instantly.

"So, do you drive Standardbreds or Morgans?" I inquired.

"Both!" they answered in unison.

And we were off, discussing the merits of synthetic harness versus leather. I turned out to be the traditionalist, since I prefer leather. They turned out to be the modern adapters, preferring synthetic for ease of maintenance. We chatted next to the heaps of rutabagas and squash, comparing the merits of old-time sharpshods (horseshoes with points for gripping ice) that I grew up with versus Drill Tec, the modern traction shoes they use. I was perfectly at ease, although perhaps they were not, since I was sporting yoga leggings and a T-shirt.

In these, as in nearly every situation and decision, the horsey aspect and possibilities have been my compass. So when it came to college, I would go, of course, where my horse could go too.

My parents, who are from small farms in Iowa, had seen little of the world except for naval bases when Dad was shipped here and there stateside during World War II. Thanks to having spent most waking hours in a barn, hayloft or pasture, I had seen much less. At sixteen, while visiting my journalist aunt in Manhattan for the first time, I made myself comfortable in the front seat of a taxi. The kind cabbie set me straight with a warning, bless him. I also asked him about "that fire at the end of the street" which turned out to be smog.

When I entered college, I knew nothing of East Coast aristocracy, whose girls attend prep schools (I'd never heard of prep schools) with names that had "The" or "Mrs." or ended in "ly". They grew up riding and went on to colleges, largely in the mid-Atlantic or the South, with names like "Briar" or "Croft" or "Fox" in them. While I was cleaning stalls and competing in 4-H, they were skiing in Zermatt or Vail. They summered in Martha's Vineyard or Kennebunkport, while my sisters and I tossed corn to pigs or gathered eggs on our grandparents' Iowa farms.

We were, superficially at least, different. Years and miles since, I have come to learn we are a sorority of worshippers, a kind of unspoken and vast club with a common language: horse.

I applied to a small private college sixty miles north of home. The town smelled like toasted grain (Malt-O-Meal cereal is milled there) and had a dream-like peace amid the oak savannah. Best of all, I could keep Gabe cheaply just five miles away with an old cowboy named Buck who raised Quarter Horses.

Freshman week, I arrived with a rented horse trailer hooked to the family

Oldsmobile. Gabe was on one side, my belongings on the other. I was accepted at what I later learned was a highly ranked college because throughout my childhood and teenage years, when I wasn't drawing horses (poorly) or designing stables (fairly well), I was reading the dictionary and studying the Reader's Digest vocabulary lists, recreating them carefully in longhand, covering one side with my palm and drilling the words over and over.

My brain was absorptive then, and multitudes of words went in that I could call up easily. Now, I must rush off and look up words I used to know, such as refulgent, hermeneutics, noisome, plangent, scry, and mnemonic. Those words were useful for the SATs and then vanished, as did the SATs. The names for types of bits, saddles, and esoteric horse breeds have stayed near the surface. If I ever have occasion to distinguish a Kladruber from a Knabstrupper, I can do it.

After graduation, keeping Gabe determined the course of my life. I did freelance writing (a little) and waitressed (a lot), trying to support myself and my horse. Then, with profound luck, a car dealership owner with several hundred acres near St. Paul, Minnesota, swapped me use of his pasture in exchange for caring for his own riding horses. I could dash from the newsroom in downtown Minneapolis, where I had landed a staff feature writing job, and in about thirty minutes switch my Calvin Kleins for Carhartts, and set off into the woods and fields.

These days, horsekeeping still dominates my life and conversations, while housekeeping is more like Pippi Longstocking, replete with a saddle in the living room, dirty riding boots on the porch and bridles on my office wall.

What remains of the me that was then?

Horses: Thinking about, talking about, fantasizing about, plotting about, weighing, comparing, wanting them. Horses are the through line, the common denominator, the default position of my waking mind. It's what links me to all horse lovers, especially horsegirls, anywhere and everywhere.

And, naturally, I have accumulated more horses, mostly as gifts.

As I meditate, cat on my lap, candle lit, the late afternoon light fading through the blinds of my living room, I am picturing riding my bay Welsh pony, leaping up and down small banks. My body, sitting cross-legged, is still, but my mind gallops with equines.

So far, I do not have horse wallpaper, horse-motif pajamas, or fluffy horsehead bedroom slippers. I do not have a toilet paper holder made from a curb bit, and my paper-towel rack is not forged from horseshoes. These and more all exist in online catalogs of the companies that serve the vast horse-crazed mostly female market. I view with amusement the football fans who have helmet-shaped mailboxes, yet how are they different from those of us who wear horsey pajamas ? How are horse-loving people different from fans of all other sports?

In part, it is because this relentless interest is not fandom, and this is not a sport. It is something more, something else, something apart. And part of the allure is that somehow horses allow me to be me, us to be us.

When did this begin? As one California horsewoman told me, "I began to love horses in the womb, when my DNA was splitting." Just so, from what I recall. It is that elemental. It is that formative. It is that pervasive and rewarding.

In November, riding at twilight through the matte gold cornfields and acres of cattails, framed by oaks gone black in the sunset, I am wearing nothing appropriate for deer opener weekend: aboard a little brown Morgan gelding, I am bundled in elderly wool sweaters and thick pull-on breeches, their various rips whipstitched into welts with my feed sack sewing skills. I am blowing my nose with one finger of my mismatched winter gloves. No blaze orange vest is needed to keep me safe, because I am in that liminal trance that rises when I have one leg on each side of a horse.

Although I know about climate chaos and political apocalypse, and although I woke up feeling creaky and unloved, for now, I feel all is well.

All is well as his unshod hooves crush the frozen, short-shorn alfalfa. All is well as we slip into the woods where deer flash among the birches, where woodpeckers dart and bob and a pair of eagles abide. All is well as we follow the side-by-side prints of a pair of coyotes in a rime of new snow.

Millions of other girls were born this way, and because it never stops, for a while, any while, in the company of horses, for us all is truly well.

CHAPTER 2

So Many Horse Books

"A learned Arab has told us that paradise on earth is to be found on the back of a horse, in the pages of a book, and in the arms of a woman. A book about horses should, then, rate as one-and-a-half terrestrial paradises, at least."

~ **George Gaylord Simpson**

This clear, sunny October day in Boston, I stroll from Harvard Yard down JFK Street heading for the Weeks Footbridge to watch a friend compete in the Head of the Charles, the biggest U.S. rowing regatta. It is an hour until the race, so as I pass the Harvard Coop, I can't resist visiting a bookstore I've never investigated.

"Where are your horse books?" I ask the young man at the information desk on the main floor.

"They'd be downstairs in the children's department," he answers.

"What about horse art or riding instruction books?" I ask.

"What we have is in the lower level."

Here on the horsey East Coast, home to American racing, steeplechasing, foxhunting, and show jumping, I am surprised that horse books are relegated to the least prestigious floor of the three-story shop. If equestrian sports are exiled from the other sports, are fishing, baseball, basketball and football (all hugely male sports) somehow more adult? Are adult horse lovers considered developmentally delayed? Is riding not sport?

Actually, I know the answer to that.

In Minnesota, my own large newspaper usually declines to cover equestrian topics in its sacrosanct sports section except, for a time, flat racing. When Minnesota had a rider contending for a spot on the Olympic equestrian team, when the top dressage stallion in the world was bred and owned by a Minnesota couple, when a Minnesota woman rode in the daunting Maryland Hunt Cup, when Crompton (Tommy) Smith, the first American jockey to win England's formidable Grand National, took a job with a Minneapolis health corporation—no coverage.

Equestrian sport is snubbed like this in many U.S. news venues, whereas in Ireland, England and other areas of the world, equestrian competition merits regular features and news coverage, sometimes even front page.

Down in the Harvard Coop basement, I squeeze into a toddler-size green Adirondack chair beneath a plastic tree flanked by a mural of rowers. On the shelves offering *The Klutz Book of Marbles* and *Let Squids Be Squids*, I find a small selection of horse books under the heading "Pets."

I open a book and am, as always, not just immersed but submerged. With horses, there is ever more to learn, and here in the kiddie corner I read delicious details, such as that Arabians have denser bones and deeper breathing passages than other breeds the better to handle long rides in the dust at high speeds in Bedouin warfare.

Prestige-less as the bookstore basement was, it may be fair shelf placement: We are introduced to horse books in childhood. And if we are hungry for horses, all the books are less than enough.

I consumed horse books avidly as a grade-school child. I gobbled up Walter Farley's *Black Stallion* series, which was followed by Anna Sewell's *Black Beauty* (1877), which I read only once; it was so painful that I could never open the pages again.

Marguerite Henry's books, *King of the Wind* (1948) in particular, struck exactly the right tone, although it made me weep in every reading as the noble Arabian stallion Sham, cast off in London, is beaten, starved, and forced to pull heavy carts. He survives with his two friends, a little Arab groom and a cat. Sham became immortal as the Godolphin Arabian, one of the foundation stallions whose speed and beauty run in the genes of Thoroughbred racehorses today.

Then, when I was about nine, I found Elizabeth Goudge's 1946 novel *The Little White Horse* in my school library. It's a tale of a horse that is probably a unicorn, a dog that is probably a lion, creatures that are probably faeries, and a venturesome English girl. I burned to own it. As the alternative, I simply signed it out, read it, returned it, and signed it out again on the spot. I assumed no one else had ever heard of it anyway. For the rest of my years at Oakwood School, my greedy strategy worked.

A decade later, when the old brick school was scheduled to be demolished, I wrote its librarian to ask if *The Little White Horse* was still there. It was, and I carried it home, placing it on a marble-topped antique dresser from our family farm. That fall, my parents put their home on a local house tour, and the next time I came home to visit, I found that someone on the tour had tucked a note into my book: "Hi, this is like seeing an old friend. Glad you have and appreciate it. It's a nice story. L. Gussner (forever) Oakwood Librarian."

More decades passed before I learned that someone else had indeed heard of it. In 2020, while digging into the subject of females and horses, I learned J.K. Rowling of *Harry Potter* fame called it her favorite book too.

Horse lovers are not just horse book lovers, but the latter are largely, hugely female.

From her horse earrings to the Celtic horse tattoo that encircles her wrist, Collette Morgan is a horsewoman as well as a top book merchant. In 2016, Wild Rumpus, her bookstore in the stylish Linden Hills neighborhood of Minneapolis, won the honor of Best Children's Bookstore in America.

The store is the domain of free-roving hens and Manx cats, of caged rats, cockatiels, and ferrets. Collette's draft cross mare, Lucy, appears as a literary consultant in the shop's newsletter "What's The Rumpus?"

"The horse book market is girls," Collette confirmed. "Reading is the closest you can get to experience horse adventures without actually doing them."

Collette and her friend Dale, a farrier (his wrist bears the same image—she calls it their "engagement tattoo") share a small herd of Gypsy horses, one of whom pulls a book wagon at special events.

Why the relationship between horses and girls? Why not dogs, cats, or, for that matter, any other companion creature?

"It's because horses have so much heart," Collette tells me over coffee around the corner from The Rumpus. "We don't have the same feeling about cows, for example. They don't have the same willingness to get along with humans."

When I discovered Wild Rumpus, its shelves were thick with series paperbacks to feed voracious young horsegirls who love books: *The Thoroughbred Series, The Saddle Club, The Short Stirrup Club*, on and formulaically on. They are written as identically as bodice rippers, those romances where curvaceous spirited girl (with great hair) meets compelling muscular boy (with great hair), boy breaks girl's heart before they are passionately reunited. Only here, it's often girl meets horse/pony (with great hair), girl loses horse/pony, and girl and horse/pony are reunited.

In addition to the horsey fiction series for tweens, teens, and toddlers (there are even horse books for three- to five-year-olds), Collette's store offered non-fiction with photos, charts, and diagrams appealing to those who want information on horse care, tack, and breeds of horses and ponies.

"When you are obsessed with a topic, you need information," Collette explained to me. "It helps you experience the thing in your head, imagine and replay it as often as you want. And if kids have the passion, the reading level doesn't matter. As we become less of a horse nation in the sense of not using them in farming, there is more horse fiction too."

Beyond bookstores, at state and county fairs, in racks at horse shows and in tack stores, I find Jody Jaffe and Carolyn Banks' equestrian mysteries, books by the late Dick Francis (former jockey to the late Queen Elizabeth and the late Queen Mother), Rita Mae Brown's Virginia hunt country mysteries, Michael Korda's witty *Horse People*, Jane Smiley's dark family drama *Barn Blind*, and Laura Hillenbrand's widely appealing true tale of champion racehorse *Seabiscuit.* Then there is *Horse* by Pulitzer-winning writer Geraldine Brooks, which to date has spent two years on the bestseller lists.

Two books written sixty-five years apart—one a novel, and one an impassioned analysis—go far toward capturing who we horsegirls are.

In the old maple nightstand next to my bed lives an early edition of Enid Bagnold's *National Velvet* acquired decades ago. One corner of the crimson and black jacket is torn away, the jacket flap shows a price of $2.50 and boasts it is a Book-of-the-Month Club selection for May 1935. The spine is stamped with silver snaffle bits. The review by William Soskin raves that this book is better than "Garbo's salary, the National Gallery, cellophane and Spring."

On the back cover is a photo, now faded to sepia, of the author aiming a chilly gaze into the camera, wearing what my mother would call a "tam" (beret). She describes Velvet Brown and her sisters as being "in the grip of horses." That is the correct term, the exact thing, the right definition of horse crazy. *National Velvet* translated unforgettably to the 1944 film starring Elizabeth Taylor (who did her own riding) and Mickey Rooney. It was nominated for several Oscars and became a TV series that ran from 1960 to 1962.

I keep a second horse book at hand, too. *Dark Horses and Black Beauties: Animals, Women, a Passion* by Melissa Holbrook Pierson ranges far and deep into literature, biology and history. Pierson's unsparing look at the brutal truths of how humans have treated and still treat horses is so disturbing (although as a journalist I cover many of them myself), I have to scurry off for comic relief to the pages of adroit literary Brits, my friends Terry Pratchett and P.G. Wodehouse and part-time Brit Bill Bryson.

Pierson reminds me that *Black Beauty*, a moral manifesto against cruelty to carriage horses, descended into the category of children's entertainment. It has, nevertheless, terrific staying power: *Black Beauty* has sold 50 million copies and continues to speak to new generations, as do periodic film remakes.

The scope and size of our hunger for horses is such that equines are the only species I know to have its own freestanding library.

In the mid-1980s, I discovered the then relatively obscure National Sporting Library (NSL) in the single-stoplight colonial village of Middleburg, Virginia. At the time, 11,000 books on equines, equine sports, and field sports were crammed in the low-ceilinged basement of Vine Hill, an 1804 red brick colonial mansion. The upper floors held the offices of *The Chronicle of the Horse* magazine, a venerable weekly with a small but intense audience of mostly competitive rider readers.

Founded in 1954 by the late Alexander Mackay-Smith (a polymath gifted in science, writing and horsemanship) and George L. Ohrstrom Sr. (owner of *The Chronicle*), the NSL is the only U.S. library of its kind. It contains material on fishing, hawking, hunting, and a bit on archery; however, the bulk of the collection concerns horses.

In this cramped cave of old and wondrous books, its then-president, Peter Winants, a tall and leggy rider, led me up and down the dim aisles.

"Dressage and foxhunting are sports where those that do it also are voracious readers," Winants told me. "NASCAR, tennis, and golf may have more participants and followers, they may get more TV coverage, but riders in general are readers."

Almost a decade after my first visit, the little library emerged from the cellar. A donation of 5,000 sporting books by John Daniels Sr. of Minnesota's Archer-Daniels-Midland Company, and the Ohrstrom Foundation's Ludwig von Hünersdorf Collection of European books on classical equitation and veterinary care necessitated the building of a new 15,000-square-foot library next door. All those reading riders with deep and often old-money pockets underwrote it. The library shares the building with a museum of sporting art, and the organizational name is now the National Sporting Library & Museum (NSLM).

The Daniels collection includes such treasures as Teddy Roosevelt's handwritten manuscript about foxhunting on Long Island in 1886 and 34 books with fore-edge paintings—images visible only when the edges of the pages are fanned.

There, I got to view one of five copies of Will James' *Smoky The Cowhorse.* On the flyleaf, James sketched himself pursued by his wife brandishing a frying pan, threatening him to get to work.

Until Virginia, I had never seen such treasures.

"Riding begets reading and the reverse," author Lawrence Scanlan, the author of *Wild About Horses,* told me. Is there a horse owner or horse lover who does not own books, follow trainers on YouTube or subscribe to a magazine on how to do it better? Is there a horse-loving reader who does not yearn to ride?

"Horses—that is to say riding—has the attribute of being a sport where people read a great deal," agreed Robin Bledsoe, longtime equestrian bookseller in Cambridge, Massachusetts. I met Robin in her shop where I staggered about, exclaiming over volumes I'd never have time to read and many I wanted to own nonetheless.

Horse addicts tend to know each other, and Robin introduced me to Fran Jurga, former editor of *Hoofcare & Lameness: The Journal of Equine Foot Science,* based in Gloucester, Massachusetts, and Dr. Castle McLaughlin, former curator of North American Ethnography at Harvard's Peabody Museum of Archaeology and Ethnology and a former board member of the Nokota Horse Conservancy.

Horse geeks and horse book geeks greater than us are few. Fran, Castle, Robin and I were grounded in the same childhood passion for ponies and identical "children's" literature.

Maureen Beebe was the first horsegirl I encountered in books. She was the young heroine of Marguerite Henry's bestselling series that began with *Misty of Chincoteague* in 1947. Wesley Dennis' graceful, airy watercolors illustrating the ponies and people of Chincoteague Island off Virginia were my favorites then and now. There was Maureen, her curly hair and polka dot dress streaming in the Atlantic coastal breeze. There were Misty and her mate, Phantom, and later their daughter, Sea Star, all whiskers and windblown pony manes and tails. I had found my herd.

Before Maureen, the only horseloving kid I knew was Alec Ramsay, the boy in *The Black Stallion* (1941), the first in Walter Farley's hit series. I knew that an Arabian stallion castaway in a shipwreck was not likely in my future. Maureen, however, was another thing, a real girl my age riding barelegged and bareback on her island pony.

I largely forgot Maureen until, decades later as a reporter interviewing celebrities on their book tours, I knocked on a Minneapolis hotel room door. A petite, fine-boned older woman opened the door. Before me stood Marguerite Henry, whose books (she had published 59 by then) had captivated me and countless other children. In addition to my notebook, my arms were full of my childhood copies of *King of the Wind* plus her books about Misty, a Grand Canyon burro named Brighty, and Justin Morgan's stallion, Figure. I looked down at their author, clutched my scuffed and dogeared volumes (as a child, I fell asleep with them) and could not hold back tears.

Our passion isn't just for books, naturally, but for film as well.

The director of the 1979 film *The Black Stallion*, Carroll Ballard, told a reporter, "I wondered for a long time, how is it that this book became such a big hit? Because I was dwelling on the old trainer and the kid talking. Stuff I thought was totally predictable. But, there is this thing. I really didn't see it for a long time. There is a mythic element in the book. It's every child's desire to have a powerful friend who can do things and who will make him powerful too. That's what's in this film. It's mythic and in the form of a black horse."

Is that it—power? Not entirely, not exactly. Mythic, certainly. Horses are not some kind of living Transformer toy, at least not for me and those I know.

The more I travel and seek, the more I inquire, listen and ponder, the more certain I am that the interpretation of our attraction as power is a largely male way of seeing horses. We dazzled girls, we smitten women, are onto something more nuanced, more complex, and more overarchingly entangled with our very nature. I aim to reveal it.

CHAPTER 3

Binding Sweethearts

"My parents...thought I would get over it. Our parents should have been right, but they were wrong. Someday, we would have boyfriends, husbands, children, careers—that's what the horses are a substitute for, according to adult theorists. For what truly horsey girls discover in the end is that boyfriends, husbands, children and careers are the substitute—for horses."

~Jane Smiley, *A Year at the Races*

Lunch hour is spent in a downtown bookstore. I edge in to the sports and outdoors magazine area, noting that it's headed, "Men's Interests" and that the fashion and home décor magazines are under the placard declaring these "Women's Interests." I paw out a copy of Arabian Horse World, thumb through it, and the hair on my arms, legs and crown of my head stands up at the images.

Sometimes I think this reaction factored into my getting married at 42, when half of Americans are well on their way to their first or second divorce.

In part, I saw no reason to be married. I had no interest in having children. I had things to do and men to do them with if I chose. I skipped both the bridal frenzy and breeding intoxication stages as they erupted around me.

In part, I saw what had befallen my mother and other women in her circle, and later even to women my age and younger: the endless domestic chores and childcare that were, and still largely are, women's assigned or default role. My high-speed mother managed to squeeze in time and achievement at golf, bowling and tennis. She never traveled on her own, however, or even much with my father. There was not enough money with three daughters to feed and clothe at Mom's standard, which was higher than the norm in our small farm town.

The various men and boys I knew rode their horses after work or on weekends, but as a child and teen, I saw no adult women riding or showing. Not one woman boarded a horse at Peterson's, Hanson's or Johnson's barns or any of the other dairy-farms-turned-boarding-barns in our county. I never saw a woman showing in regional horse show classes or at the county fairs.

That was then. It has changed radically, of course. Women are the bulk of horse boarders now, as they are also the majority of veterinary college students and equine vets.

So I wanted my own money and mobility as badly as anything, and when I got those, thanks to a newspaper job starting in my twenties, I did everything my parents had not done: watched the sunset in French Polynesia, sailed the Aegean, river rafted in Brazil, helicopter hiked in the Canadian Rockies. I worked, I traveled, and I supported myself and my horse.

Adventure and independence were and are paramount to me. Men came and went, often tumultuously. Through all this, the gray Arabian named Gabe was my "binding sweetheart."

Novelist and poet Jim Harrison gave me the term. I interviewed him the first time in a Minneapolis motel where he was staying while on a book tour. We discussed his interests: hunting, Michigan, writing, food, Chinese poets and other poets. I mentioned horses, Gabe in particular, who was by then quite elderly.

Gabe died the subsequent April. In October, I married someone I inarguably should not have. When the flower girl walked down the aisle that bright day in a country church on a breezy hilltop, she carried a small gray model Arabian in her basket of autumn blooms. A memento to Gabe, a totem, a sign that I was not giving up horses.

When Jim came around on another book tour, I was again his interviewer. I told him Gabe was gone.

Not long afterward, his *After Ikkyu and Other Poems* was published. The fifty-first of fifty-seven poems began thus: *"A lovely woman in Minnesota owned a 100-year-old horse, actually 37, but in horse years that's at least a 100."*

Jim took a poet's license, of course. Gabe died at 28, not 100 or 37. And I knew with a deep, quiet pleasure, that my beloved now lived in a poem, which continues:

"In the third grade I read there were eleven surviving
Civil War veterans. Under the photo captions it said
they were mostly drummer boys. Now both
the horse and veterans are dead, the woman married, rid
of her binding sweetheart horse. I know these
peculiar
things because I'm Jim, at the right place, the right time."

I also know that "rid" is not quite the word; our bonds with what girls and women have come to call their "heart horse" never release. Gabe was mine. I was his. Horsewomen and girls now also talk about meeting our beloved animals again "over the rainbow bridge." May it be so for all of us who love these creatures in this way.

Binding sweethearts now populate pastures and stables all over the country and other countries as more women can afford the time, money, and effort to keep a horse. Fundamentally, too, is that more of us now feel entitled to our own passions.

"Sometimes I feel kind of guilty that I am passionately in love with this," said Carole, who competes in hunter jumper classes with her two off-the-track Thoroughbreds. She was a married 30-something attorney when I met her, and she rode six days a week—even more than I did.

"I wonder what people think of me," she said. "I don't have kids, and they must look at my life and think, 'What an incredibly narcissistic person!' Nobody has confronted me about it, it's just a sense. I sometimes wish I wanted kids so I could be 'normal.' I was raised in a fundamentalist church that was very repressive toward pleasure, but it didn't stop me. I rebelled. I do recognize that I'm very lucky to be able to do this, that I fit it into my life, that I have the income to support horses. Sometimes I think I'm having too much fun."

Back to the magazines, which reveal much.

Reading a horse magazine, I spot an ad: "16.2 h bay Warmblood/Arab mare. Athletic, elegant, extravagant movement. Rides and drives. Priced to sell at $7900, owner getting married." And in a newsletter, I spot an ad from an Iowa woman: "Big beautiful half-Arabian gelding, 7 yr. 15.2 h, good dressage prospect, excellent on trails, calm, has been in several clinics, trailed cattle in Wyoming. Getting married, have to sell. Good home only."

Nowhere do I see ads for men selling their golf clubs because they are getting married or men shedding their motorboats or Harleys because of impending nuptials. They may acquire wives but get to keep their "sweethearts."

This probably isn't a financial decision. I doubt the horse is being sold to pay for the wedding. It's a shift in focus for the woman selling the athletic gelding or the fine mare. It's a lifestyle and social change consented to—under what terms? Does anyone even negotiate? I'll give up the horse, honey, if you sell that snowmobile?

I want to call the women posting the ads and urge them not to marry the guy if it's a that-horse-or-me decision. I hope they would marry the kind of man who buys them a horse or a saddle or even a horse trailer for their birthday, anniversary, or Christmas, or no reason at all except he respects what he can never replace.

And with which he can never compete: I married after a tumultuous eight-year courtship. It was the wrong person for the wrong reasons but a heckuva wedding, replete with a team of Percherons and a pair of mules each pulling a surrey.

A few years later, after a concussion from falling on a winter sidewalk, I had dizzy spells. I tried to ignore them, but that spring, after falling off (more surprised than hurt, as it had been decades since I'd hit the ground) several times in one week, I decided to give in and buy a saddle. Until then I had ridden largely bareback, which was both easy and comfortable. I settled on a used dressage saddle whose soft leather and long stirrup flaps kept the sensation as close to riding bareback as I could find. It was on consignment in a local tack shop; when I asked the shop owner why it was for sale, she told me the seller had just had her first child.

I carried off the saddle not without some sadness. A woman had sold her saddle, and presumably her horse as well, because she had a baby. I could not imagine that choice. For a brief while, my elation with the saddle was a bit wilted by its origins: is our choice men and children, or some sort of alternate intimacy with a horse? Do we create that equation or do we succumb to something expected by (some) males, by society, by simple economics and scarcity of time?

Horses are not some sort of vaccination against romantic human attraction. (Ask my ex-husband.) They are not equivalent or comparable or a surrogate. Despite what some men think, they are actually not rivals. They are something other, and they fill an inarticulable need. In them, we always have a true companion, a steadying counterweight to more complicated and sometimes problematic relationships with people. (Again, just ask any horsewoman's ex.)

No survey has looked in depth at the marital status of the members of the horse community, but I am intrigued by anecdotes and observations. Reflecting on some of the women I met in my search for the answer to who, what, and why we are horse lovers, I find: Susan Franklin, never married, no children; Kim McElroy, never married, no children; Karen Lancaster, married, no children; Suzanne Drenec, divorced, no children; Dr. Kathy Ott, married, no children; Michele Delong Reiter, married, no children; Nan Cowin, partnered, no children; Lyn Cowan, single, no children; Phyllis Dawson, divorced, no children; Anita White, married, step-children; Norma Vermeer, divorced, one child; Cat Joachim, single, no children; Carol Federighi, married, no children; Betsy Philips, married, no children; Jeannie Cassells, married, no children; Anna Blake, married, no children.

Of course, I know horsewomen who have horsey daughters and granddaughters, too. In some families, it goes on through generations, supported, encouraged, and even shared with mates.

A 1994 reader survey by *The Chronicle of the Horse* (COTH) showed 85 percent of the 22,000 subscribers were female with an average age of 41. Fifty-seven percent were married and 36 percent had children.

When I checked in 2024, the Chronicle had gone digital as well as print, logging more than 7.6 million website page views per month. It has 407,000 Facebook followers and a 76 percent female readership.

They no longer track marital status, said Linda Andersen, COTH's director of marketing. She speculates, however, that since "this is a consuming passion and lifestyle," many of the readers are "moms to horses and not humans."

I don't feel like a horse's mother, although lately I hear many women refer to themselves that way. I don't feel my horse is my mate in any conventional or even unconventional sense.

It is something else. What?

CHAPTER 4

The Twelve-Hundred-Pound Muscle

"Well that's hogwash! To me there's absolutely nothing sexual about being in a barn with a million flies, manure, and a horse dragging you around, a horse that wants attention. If men think it's about sex, they should come out and watch for half an hour."

~ **Nan Cowan,** ***saddle shop co-owner***

A winter solstice celebration in an elegant old Minneapolis neighborhood. Writers, artists, politicians, and music promoters circulate, sipping champagne. A dining room table swagged in ivory lace offers antique silver platters of rare roast beef, dilled salmon and cold shrimp. Glossy and delicate tortes, cascades of fresh pomegranates, figs and nuts beckon from the sideboard.

I arrive near midnight after five hours of driving carriages in the snow in downtown St. Paul, a profitable shift in bustling holiday traffic. After loading the Percherons in their owner's trailer and rolling the carriages away into a storage garage, I rush home, change and set out for the party.

Now, in a candlelit alcove, I am talking with the editor of a national magazine and a painter, one an old friend, one a social acquaintance.

When the men ask where I've been and I tell them, a sly, silly glaze creeps across both their faces. They suddenly look like two Great Danes in evening dress, their forepaws on the table, ears pricked. I imagine ropey saliva dribbling from their jowls.

"What is it with women and horses?" one says, averting his eyes from my face. This is not a question, it is a pretext for the two of them to run images across their mental movie screens.

"Well, I guess it's hard to resist a 600-pound muscle between your legs," says the other. They grin, tightly.

I want to say "Draft horses, guys: 1800 pounds, sometimes 2200 pounds. You're obsessed with size? Take that!"

It is a fine party, however, an evening swimming in the pale gold aura of good conversation, comfort and plenty. So I behave myself, although I steam silently inside my party clothes and party manners.

They'd done it again: defined horses by a measure that many men use in the ongoing comparison they make between horses and themselves, as if horses are in some way their rivals.

I've encountered this kind of sniggering from men in my former newsroom, men at meetings, men at my own dinner parties. When horses are mentioned, there is a visible shift as they are suddenly riveted by obvious erotic thoughts, thoughts I don't have when I ride or think about horses. Thoughts I certainly never had about Gabe in nearly three decades together. Thoughts no female I've known has when she rides.

At best, it shows a tedious and willful inability to understand. At worst, it degenerates into leering quips about Catherine the Great and a sort of sexual itchiness that sabotages the conversation.

They (non-riding men) assume or maybe hope that we (horsewomen) are unusual in some prurient way—more sexually voracious, more viscerally wired.

"Horsewomen are supposed to be better in bed—that's what men think," said my riding teacher Judy, stubbing out a cigarette in disgust and rolling her eyes. We were sitting in the tack room of a country stable where she taught and trained. Judy had worked for twenty years on the American Saddlebred and Morgan show circuits. This was the rumor among many men she encountered, she said.

I fail to see the connection: is there such a rumor about, say, male swimmers or skiers or table tennis players?

Imagine the reverse with women describing a man (with apologies to Monty Python):

"Hey, you know he golfs," (nudge, nudge, wink, wink). "I bet he really likes to go."

Or, "you know, that guy really likes (knowing pause) fishing," (throat clearing, blushing, fidgeting.)

Maybe, I think, this is just primordial rivalry, men placing themselves in opposition to animals who are utterly oblivious to the competition.

Maybe it's a case of distorted competitiveness, an equation where animal= nature=threat. It puzzles me perpetually, just as I am annoyed each time I hear or read men using such expressions as "taming nature" and "conquering the savage wilderness."

Perhaps it's a matter of mass, some Paleolithic remnant of a neurological need to take on bigger forces that frighten them.

I brought that up to writer Rita Mae Brown, a horsewoman and novelist, when I contacted her at her Virginia farm, where she writes her popular Sneaky Pie Brown series among others. What's the difference in our approach to horses, I asked her.

"Did you see the NSL's [National Sporting Library] exhibit of ancient Greek vases?" she asked me. "Even then and there, the women owned the horses, but they were not on horses. It showed the representation of a different relationship: the horse was looking at the woman, whereas men led or were controlling them. Women are much more sensible about not trying to muscle 1,200-pound animals. Boys are taught to take charge of things. With horses, you can't take charge, and unless you are a complete idiot, you don't try. Women start off trying to cooperate; we figure maybe there is another way."

One evening at my carriage driving job, I was driving high school prom couples around downtown St. Paul. My horse that night was Karen, a black Percheron mare with four white socks and a blaze, some 1,800 pounds of easygoing, cuddly, motherly calm and goodwill. When she is not at work, she lowers her broad, gentle face, places a nostril on my cheek, and breathes tenderly on me in big moist horse sighs.

We rolled slowly past a bus stop where a dozen men and boys loitered. They seemed to confuse size with virility, and none of them knew enough to discern that big, sweet Karen, struggling to hold the carriage steady on that sloping pavement, was a mare.

There were hoots and shrieks and snorts and unmistakable guffawing about penis size in gutter language. Karen could not blush, but I did—for the horse, for me, and for the young couples in my carriage. I wanted to take my carriage whip to the whole crowd.

Horses sexy? Certainly, in the American sense of sexy as an amalgam of power, beauty and desirability. The way certain cars are sexy, maybe, or good fabric, or beautiful packaging. But horses as sexual, supplanting males in some sort of interspecies *amour*?

When I discussed this with Julie Suhr, who holds records in the hundred-mile Tevis Cup, the top endurance race in North America, she was in her seventies and still riding her adored Arabian horses. She had literally put in thousands of miles over boulders, down ravines, across deserts on horseback, and she growled at the idea that our attraction to equines is in any way sexual.

"When I was a three-year-old girl, I knew I wanted to ride the rest of my life," she told me. "How is that sexual? That's not true."

What we believe about our attraction to horses has a vast chasm, and some men fill it with misinformation. It's more about the onlooker, the viewer, than the looked-at, the viewed, I've come to believe.

One July day that began with a man yelling, "Yeah, baby," at me in the food co-op parking lot as I bent over to pick up litter, ended with a man in a grocery store (when you ride, you can eat anything and I go from feeding to feeding) coming from essentially the same place. The latter was wearing a T-shirt that featured the cover of his new book about schizophrenia. I noticed this by the deli counter, where he and his wife were also selecting dinner, and we began talking about books. I could see his topic on his shirt, so I told him mine, not that he asked.

"Girls and women and their relationship to horses, that huge attraction that many of us have," I said. "I've been talking with psychiatrists, psychologists, anthrozoologists, sociologists…"

"I'm a psychiatrist: It's about sex," he interrupted, dismissively.

"That's what some men think, and it's wrong," I said, turning away quickly so I didn't say more. Stuffing a chocolate bar into my mouth on the drive home, I fumed: "Simplistic, reductionist, archaic, condescending. Not everything you put between your legs is about what's between your legs. Not everything is displacement. Are you suggesting that my two smashed ankles, several concussions, financial fragility, near-daily devotions decade after decade are about sex? You, sir, have told me more about your lack of imagination, depth, and perception than about female love of horses."

And yet, some men get it. My father, for one.

I was about six years old, maybe younger. When Dad arrived home from work to our one-story rambler with its Danish modern furniture and blond hi-fi with big gold mesh speakers, I was waiting. The carpet—beige, wall-to-wall, nylon—was so synthetic that my younger sister and I had "shock fights" on it, scooting our stocking feet until we built up a charge, then touching each other with the subsequent spark and shrieking. I was, as always, really just waiting for Dad.

He was my horse, and when he passed through the door, I begged to "play horse!"

Dad took off his suit coat and tie, rolled up the sleeves of his starched white shirt and got down on his hands and knees. I mounted up, gripped hard with my legs, and kicked him in the ribs. It would have felt too intimate to hang on to his hair, which was light brown, wavy and nicely combed, so I rode with seat and legs.

I demanded bucks, I demanded trots, and he maneuvered from the glossy black Hammond organ to the blond coffee table and back, grunting "Oof!" until it was time for dinner. He was my pony until a year or two later, when he provided me with Molly. My father, who had grown up on a farm riding horses, never thought of my horse love as a substitute for anything else. He just made it all possible.

I took the question to Maxine Kumin, a Pulitzer-winning poet, essayist, and horsewoman, who writes that "the old stereotype about girls and horses has always seemed to me too facile to be trusted."

Kumin believes horse love is more abundant among girls on the East Coast, while in the West, a cowboy-flavored horse fever (never equated with sex, I notice) abounds in boys as well. She also distrusts the Freudian concept "because it does not adequately explain the substantial number of adult females who, despite their comfortable adaptation to sex roles involving marriage and child rearing, continue to lease, own, care for, ride and/or raise horses."

Horses and girls may be a good match, she writes, because horses offer girls a measure of control at a stage in their lives when much seems out of control. "When all else shifts, changes, and disappoints, the horse can remain her one constant."

In the preface to *Cowgirl Rising*, a collection of paintings by Donna Howell-Sickles, Teresa Jordan, author of *Cowgirls: Women of the American West*, writes about the special bond between girls and horses and about the characteristic and common male distortion of it.

"I remember a college friend, a psychology major, once telling me this connection is Freudian, which is to say sexual," Jordan said. "He went on to suggest that the reason many girls grow away from horses in adolescence is that the sexuality becomes too obvious, too embarrassing. In later years, after their marriages have cooled, women often find their interest in horses reignited."

"I listened to my friend, but I didn't believe him," she writes. "Horses are beautiful and strong and certainly there is something erotic about them. But if it were a matter of—I still remember his phrase—'that throbbing manlife between the legs,' girls would be drawn to motorcycles. I think girls bond with horses because horses don't diminish them. Horses don't coo over them because they are cute, or shun them because they aren't cute enough. They don't judge them for being too rowdy or too quiet, too skinny or too fat. Horses respond to something deeper, to essence and intention. When a ninety-pound girl and a nine-hundred-pound horse canter through a reining pattern together, they have developed a mutual respect and honest communication that few girls can find anywhere else."

As a child, I was never embarrassed about my fondness for horses, never reluctant to talk horses because of how it would be misconstrued or "too obvious" or too anything. That onus, that smirking disapprobation, landed on me in my late teens.

I saw the change first in the way men looked at me.

For years, a skinny little girl with lank blond hair riding a pony was beneath their notice. Their eyes skidded away, vague, uninterested.

But a girl of sixteen or older was a different matter. I was startled to see that drooling hound look, a look that seemed to carry keener hunger because I was on a horse. I began to be glad that Gabe was nimble and fast when those looks came at me over lowered car windows or from under motorcycle helmets.

Perhaps the confusion is understandable. My language about riding and horses, when I look at it, is passionate. What language do we have for ardent love of another living creature except that which sometimes verges on the erotic?

My voice lifts up into little cooing grace notes when I speak to cats or dogs or anything warm-blooded. Talking to Gabe and to other horses—the universal refrain is, "What a good boy!" "What a good girl!"—deserves a different language, but what are our choices?

What language do we have to express this kind of love? Neither the sugary, simpleminded baby talk we shower on human infants nor the language of adult erotic love seem right.

Call it falling in love, but I am goofy about equids of all ages, sexes, and levels of dignity: the nippy baby zebra with the woolly back; a silvery donkey with yard-long ears and weird, raw, quavering haws; the affable bay mule who carried me lightly around a noisy ring.

Just don't call it lust.

"It's not sexual at all!" said Muffy Seaton, winner of multiple national competitive driving championships with her Dartmoor ponies. At her farm in South Carolina, she trains driving pairs and four-in-hand ponies. "It's like sailing, that free power, especially in a boat with a tiller, the same feeling. It's also a nurturing thing. And it's comforting to be with a horse: I'm sheltered here. Then there's their honesty and willingness to do things with you—they are dead honest; to me that's the most important thing."

This may not be marriage, but it is love, and it is certainly a mating, a kind of interspecies soul-bond. The loss of this partner, many women tell me, is, frankly equal to or far greater than any other loss except perhaps that of a child.

Men think about sex many times an hour, or so we're told by researchers. Perhaps believing themselves the norm, they can't conceive of women thinking of horses that many times an hour without it being sexual. Surely this must be some kind of sublimation, the thinking runs, for the "normal" female desire to be with them.

I assumed it was only some straight men who held this view until one evening in a theater lobby I ran into a gay man I'd known for years. We exchanged pleasantries, and I told him about my work.

"Well, little girls and horses..." he said knowingly, taking up invisible reins and miming a rider moving her pelvis pleasurably.

"Ick," I thought and turned away.

As regards women and horses, Freud and others have sexual theories, but they are off the mark, says Dr. Elizabeth Lawrence, cultural anthropologist at Tufts University. Lawrence, who passed away in 2003, was also a veterinarian and specialist in animal–human relationships.

"It may have that element about it, but it's not that," she told me. "It's some kind of interactive reaching out to another species. I don't agree with Freud or any of those who say it is sexual movement of your body. Men say that, and many of them are kind of envious of this kind of relationship."

To an (overtly and covertly) androcentric world, an intense relationship outside of that paradigm must be chiseled to fit. Why is a girl or woman's relationship with a horse so often interpreted as a surrogate for a male or a baby? Why is it not a thing unto itself, *sui generis*, with its own beauty and power?

In the main arena of the Equine Affair, a horse exposition in Columbus, Ohio, the sold-out two-hour Saturday evening show featured a variety of horses performing to music: Quarter Horses in metallic streamers and glitter, Thoroughbreds in American flag blankets, Trakehners in improvised horse tuxedos and bow ties. With one or two exceptions, all riders and handlers were female. Puzzlingly to me, twice the music used for the acts was "I Need a Hero" and once "I'm Your Man." No wonder our love is conflated with human desire.

I have never heard a girl or a woman speak about horses as erotic, however, although sex can enter into the equation in other ways.

A woman in Tampa, Florida, told me that among her wealthy friends, "the fathers bought the girls horses to keep them virgins—and it worked."

This attitude is not new. In the 16th century, vigorous horseback riding was among the exercises recommended by physicians for "female hysteria," a euphemism for what was misinterpreted (again, by the male medical establishment) as frustrated erotic desire.

For the most part, I suspect the common inability to conceive of a love that is not erotic derives from a largely phallocentric world view. Many men seem to consider themselves an inevitability in a woman's life, and some of them see horses as a deviation from them.

Gary, a Sausalito, California, Thoroughbred trainer turned TV sound man, told me men believe horses are like dolls, something for girls to outgrow.

"Little girls play with dolls, with toy horses, they draw horses," said Gary. "To men, horses are toys. When women get married, many men I know tell them to grow up, give up the toys."

I look at my geldings, Smokey, Shadow, Darcy and Bailey, and know that I find their warm, sleek hides sensual, their breath alluring, their ears enticing. When my friends Lucy, Sally, Sarah, Laurie and I share stories about horses, we adore their senses of humor, we lament their foibles, and we praise their rumps and necks and noses. The adoration is not the same as whatever more complicated emotions we may feel for men or for other women or any human, for that matter.

Nor is it simply a hunger for power. If it were, women would go out and do what some men with a power craving do: invest in a motorcycle, sports car, a cigarette boat, a monster truck or their equivalents.

On good days, when our horses come running at our call, our hearts leap up. We cannot help ourselves. In horse territory, on horseback, we roam beyond physical desire and in the dimension of a pure love.

CHAPTER 5

Secret Horses

"Women love horses better than they love men."
-Erica Jong, *Sappho's Leap*

My horse habit is out in the open, sometimes embarrassingly so. I was shocked, however, to learn that other women, lots of other women, sneak off to see their horses. Some siphon off dollars from the grocery money to keep their forbidden best friend, their secret soul buddy, their horse.

I first found this out from Nan, a horsewoman who ought to know: she and her partner Cindy encountered many surreptitious horsewomen.

For two decades, Nan and Cindy owned a saddle shop in White Bear Lake, Minnesota. Once one of the two English tack stores in the state and still one of the largest dressage and hunt saddleries in the upper Midwest, it attracts a 99.9 percent female clientele from Iowa, the Dakotas and Wisconsin, as well as Minnesota and online from well beyond the Midwest.

I visited their shop almost weekly, the pretext being needing a saddle pad or a brush or to sit in one of the used saddles on consignment. The steadying aroma of saddle leather greeted me at the door. Inside, I clambered onto saddles that would put me literally in the more-saddle-than-horse category and pawed through books, boots, and bits while snacking on chocolate medallions embossed with horse heads.

With horse manure particles crumbling off my salt-stained boots, squashed wood ticks under my nails, and holes in my riding tights, I was not their average customer. Those tended to be neatly dressed mothers with pre-teen or teen daughters or sleek middle-aged dressage riders with tidy hair, shining boots, and spotless breeches with full-suede seats.

One morning, Nan and I met over coffee at a nearby shop to talk about her special—but apparently not entirely unusual—clientele.

A lean, middle-aged woman with short silver hair and shy dark eyes, Nan looked the part of a dressage rider: all restraint, quiet elegance and understatement.

"About forty percent of our customers have horses that no one else knows about," she told me as the mocha steam rose around us. "These are women from all walks of life. It's not just an issue of economics. It's an issue of families who don't want to know their wife or mother has something other than them."

I was astonished. I still am.

Having grown up with encouragement from my father to ride and taken my horse to college with me, I knew I was far luckier than the norm, but I had assumed that adult women in this century and in this country at least were allowed their own interests.

Not so, Nan said. At least, not this interest.

The women she knew who hide their habit generally work full time, she added, yet make time to visit a horse stashed somewhere.

"Some go see their horses at 5:30 in the morning—I don't know what excuses they give about why they aren't home," she said.

They are also resourceful about paying for horse supplies.

"Many times, they ask us 'Can I write the check to cash?' or they pay in cash, often in one-dollar bills, probably grocery and gas change. They don't buy a huge ticket item all at once, they put it on lay-by forever. Their payments are regular, $10 here and $5 there, and finally, they get whatever the prized possession is."

Selling them bridles and riding bras, saddles, and liniment, Nan hears her clients' secrets the way hairdressers do. Women with secret horses have several things in common, Nan noted; among them, a spouse who doesn't want his wife spending much time away from him. Some of the men can and do go to extremes, she added.

"We have a client whose husband won't let her go out after dark, another whose husband wants her to be available no matter what, so she always has to carry a beeper and a cellphone," she said, her pale face calm as I sputtered into my coffee.

"No! Why?" I asked her.

"It's hard for me to imagine," she replied.

Some believe their horse is a luxury they don't deserve, she said, but love compels them to harbor their horses despite the guilt and secrecy.

"They can't *not* have their horses, they won't give them up," Nan explained. "And these are not horses kept in splendor. They are well cared for but kept in basic situations. The time the women can spend with them is minimal. The time they'd like to spend is a lot more. These are husbands who have jobs where they are really engrossed, and when they come home they have dinner and watch TV or play video games or read the paper or work. It's not like there's a lot they do together when they get home."

What's at stake is more than an issue of time. These same men presumably don't forbid their wives cats, dogs or other pets.

"There's something about a woman being able to deal with a half-ton animal that is always amazing, and I think to some people, that can be really threatening," she surmised, confirming what I had experienced as well. "Some of the men have their own fears about horses and how big they are; that their wife has no fear of horses is threatening to them."

Shortly after I spoke with Nan, I had a glimpse of exactly what she had told me. I had started a Shire cross filly (a young female part-draft horse) for a friend and was advertising her for sale. A woman called to make a date to see the filly.

"When you call my house, just leave your name and number, don't say what it's about," said Sue. "I don't want my husband to know. He used to support the idea, but now he doesn't really like it."

Several years ago, when their three children were all under age five, Sue explained, her husband endorsed her having a horse. Given the age of the children, I thought to myself, that endorsement seemed largely theoretical. Now that the children are older, and she is actually shopping for one, he disapproves, she said.

"Does your husband golf?" I asked her.

"Oh yes, but he works very hard, I wouldn't ask him not to golf."

"No, I mean, he has a sport, why would he resent you having your own recreation?" I said.

"He thinks it will take away from my family time," she said. She came to see the filly and loved her but didn't buy her. To this day, I don't know if she ever got her own horse. I hope so.

As much as there are couples who share a love of horses, who ride trails together, who compete together in everything from team penning to fox chasing, who grieve together over a horse's passing, there are those where a male fears a shortage of love and attention if a woman has an interest in horses.

"Many men don't like horsewomen because they know they will always be second to their horses," my friend Tabea Brock told me. We were strolling the aisles at the annual Minnesota Horse Expo one April day in St. Paul, scratching the necks of Fjord horses, stroking the velvet muzzles of mules, admiring the mighty haunches of Percherons, the cascading feathers of Shires and applauding the antics of foals.

Tabea is the equine operation manager of We Can Ride, a therapeutic riding program, and holds an instructor certificate from a German equestrian society.

"I came here with a dog, two suitcases and a thousand dollars, I didn't speak the language. I left my horses behind in Germany."

After working in elder memory care for seven years, Tabea ached to get back to the horse world. By then, however, she was married.

"I missed them so much, I would give anything to see and smell a horse, so I started to ride again and soon friends at the barn began saying 'you need your own horse.' My husband would never let me, he said it was too much money, too much time, too stinky. I didn't have the money, but friends loaned me the money. So Bubbles, a yearling Gypsy foal, was my secret for six months. Then I felt it would be the right thing to do to tell him, because now he knows it's clean and no additional money. So I sent him a cute letter from Bubbles with a photo of her and telling how she is sweet and loves to do tricks. When I came home that night, he started throwing things, he ripped up the cute picture and letter. He printed up divorce papers he found on line. And he told me 'I am done with you! It will be all about the horse!"

"Bubbles saved my life," said Tabea, who is now the unofficial resident expert at Horse Play, a stable in Corcoran, Minnesota, where there are 62 boarders, two of them men. In addition to Bubbles, she has two donkeys and a mule. "When I meet men and tell them I have animals, the guys always say 'we know horsewomen, it's all about the horse: the love goes to the horse, the money, the weekends, the nights are the horse.'"

"Now I have a happy heart and an empty wallet," she says. "But if I die tomorrow I die happy."

Like Tabea and the 60 women who board their horses with hers, it is largely female horse owners—covert or overt, recreational or competitive—who fuel the equine and equestrian goods market in most areas of the country. Many of them delicately adjust the equation of love, money and time to accommodate partners and families.

Linda Chiaramonte works at The Riding Store in the Chicago suburb of Woodridge. Here, too, the clientele is almost exclusively women—98 to 99 per cent according to store owner Susan Musaus, a dressage rider.

"They don't hide their horses, but many women don't want to let their husbands know how much they spend on them," Linda told me. "Women come in all the time and say, 'Put part on Visa, and I'll pay this part in cash, so my husband won't know.' Others have husbands who will buy anything for their wives, who dote on them. But a lot of them hide what they spend."

"There's a bit of rivalry between men and their wives' horses; I pick this up all the time," said Linda. "I felt it when I had both a horse and a husband. It's like they try to be real supportive, but you get this underlying hint you're paying too much attention to the horse and not enough to them."

Like marital infidelity, the secret seems to come out at awkward moments and in shocking ways.

One spring day, I arranged to ride on rounds with Dr. Kathy Ott, a veterinarian and show jumper rider with a clinic in a Twin Cities suburb. Kathy is lean and leggy, with a kind of unflappable calmness and candor I have grown used to seeing in veterinarians.

During the usual stops for teeth floating (dental work), de-worming and vaccinations, I helped hold horses for her, and we talked about her heavily female clientele.

"I have run across women who keep their horses secret, usually from their husbands," Kathy agreed. "In one case, I didn't realize the horse was a secret: the woman had other horses, but she hadn't told her husband she'd bought a pregnant mare. When he received our bill for the foaling, he called and said, 'We don't own a horse by that name or a mare with a foal.' Then we called the wife, and she said, 'He doesn't know we own the horse. Call and tell him it's a mistake.' I was in a quandary, because I had to ask my office staff to lie. The bill should have gone to her, so in a way it was a mistake, so I said to the staff to just say we mistakenly billed you."

"It's beyond me how and why somebody could hide something like that," said Kathy. "They not only own it, but they have a responsibility for it. I don't see how they could hide it from their husbands, but it does happen. It's a control issue, financial in some situations; the husband wants to be in charge of how the finances are spent and how many horses are kept. The woman doesn't have the ability or courage to stand up to him. Instead, she does it on the sly."

I wondered if women with secret horses are particularly cut off from power; not just financial power, but power in a relationship. Nan and Kathy suggested that often the women with hidden horses don't have a career or are not bringing in money equal to their partner's income.

For a silent moment or three, as Kathy turned her pickup truck down a driveway to treat another woman's backyard horse, we two child-free career women reveled in our luck and our choices.

"I think it is unfortunate when women don't have a source of income or their own spending money," she said. "Sometimes, the husband knows his wife has a horse, but the wife doesn't want him to know how much money is spent on it. There are a lot of situations where a stable manager (also a woman) will tell me, 'Do not bill this client; we will write you a check, but her husband cannot know about it.' At various stables, we have clients on file with a note: 'Husband does not know about this horse.'"

Then there are happy accommodations to the love of horses. Her own husband, a fellow vet in their clinic, is that kind of partner.

"He knew when we started dating how important horses are to me and never tried to get in the middle of my relationship with horses in any way," she told me. "When we decided to have the wedding outdoors, I knew he didn't really want to get married on horseback, because he's not much of a rider, but he said, 'I know you really want the horse in the wedding, so why don't we have your horse give you away?'"

To guitar accompaniment, her show jumper, a chestnut 17-hand Thoroughbred gelding named Roger Rabbit, walked her down the grassy aisle sporting red ribbons in his mane and tail.

"He usually walks fast, but he was very stately and walked slowly, looking around," she said. "When we got to the front, I handed his lead rope to a friend. That said I'm giving up part of my commitment to my horse and now giving part of my commitment to my husband."

Who loves horses like this, like we do? Who loves them enough to hide them if necessary? Who are we, the women who won't give them up?

CHAPTER 6

Following a Cloud

"The aisle was full of horses and ponies standing on cross ties and little girls attending them. Every one of them had that look of a girl infatuated with horses, the happy, fated look of a passenger setting sail on the Titanic."

~ Jane Smiley, *Horse Heaven*

"Look, it's Custer!"

In the twilight shadows on the steep mountain slope, a small blue roan Mustang trots through the stunted pines, moving urgently, like a teenager left by his gang—"Hey guys, wait for me! Wait up!"

Light snow is falling at 8,000 feet where we stood with binoculars watching the Pryor Mountain Range Mustang bands thread down the mountain.

He had stayed out late in the early twilight, and now Custer ran, following by scent the route of his family, turning sharply on the narrowing path, seeking the stallion named Plenty Coups and his band.

"Custer is a three-year-old who should have been kicked out," explained Ginger Kathrens, an Emmy-Award-winning PBS documentary filmmaker who tracks wild horses in Mongolia as well as here on the top of Wyoming.

When I met her at a lower altitude just a few hours earlier, I was taken with her startling blue eyes and curly blond hair in a face of refined sharpness. Now, we were bashing along the top of the Pryor Mountain Wild Horse Range in her green Jeep, her camera gear stashed amid a welter of camping supplies.

Her dog, Cola, was perched with us among the jiggling and sloshing food and water jugs and enough wine for a regiment. We were going to overnight at Pen's cabin, a century-old shelter, and watch the wild families as long as the weather held.

Ginger knows more about wild horses than almost any other man or woman alive, having spent decades following and filming them. While I wanted a pretext to see wild bands, I also wanted to know what it is about wild horses that inspires this woman and many others to volunteer to protect the horses on their dwindling range.

"There's Cloud!" she points down into a coulee where six young stallions quietly wend their way through the pines, heading toward the waterhole below us.

The soil here is pinky-red, and Cloud, a pale palomino, is salmon-colored from rolling in it. He loafs with his buddies, gently nibbling dry grasses and forbs. The six bachelors are showing the beginnings of thick winter coats. They will need them: winter comes hard and early up here.

Ginger waves to him—"Hi, it's me"—more symbolically than anything, and the herd does not spook or even take notice.

Here, high in the realm of so-called wild horses, I notice their eyes are anything but wild. The wildness I have seen in horse eyes has been in the show ring, in the auction arena, on the trail. I have seen desperation, defiance, mischief, fear, affection and amusement in horses' eyes. Here, through binoculars chilly on my cheeks, I see their lowered necks, their mild faces and their sedate and gentle movements. They are where they should be, doing what they should do.

The snow lifts, the day warms, and families are napping: first, a foal named Thunder folds his legs and lies down in the noon sun, then the mare, then the stallion. Horses lie down only when they are relaxed, secure and trusting.

Ginger and I lie down, too, watching them through binoculars and the mammoth lenses of her cameras. At this elevation—about 8,000 feet—I'm glad for a rest in the cold, dry air.

"I find more rewards in this than any other project," she tells me, and I can see why.

There are debates about the terms "wild" and "feral" and their legal protections, but either way, we are surrounded by 40,000 acres designated in 1968 as the Pryor Mountain Wild Horse Range, the first wild horse refuge in the U.S. and our largest documented wild horse herd. The Pryor horses are one of a small number of bands: the Kiger in Oregon, the Sulphur in western Utah, and the Cerbat in Arizona. Custer and his kin are perhaps the most-studied group of wild horses in the country, in no small part thanks to Ginger's work photographing and documenting them.

"This is the only wild North American herd whose factor in their blood type reveals a link to the horses of the Caribbean, horses whose ancestors rode trans-Atlantic in small galleons with Spanish invaders 500 years ago," she explains, citing research by Dr. Gus Cothran at the University of Kentucky in Lexington. "They go back to the Sorraia, a Spanish breed. The National Biological Service confirms the horses in the Pryors are unique."

I have seen and ridden Spanish horses, albeit the more modern type, and in the horses of the Pryor bands, I recognize the sloping rump, the hefty, short cannon bones, the shapely head and neck, the proud carriage, and the compactness of Spanish horses.

Who are the advocates for them and the other wild ones, I ask Ginger.

"Almost everybody I work with on this issue is a woman," Ginger tells me. "There are two male biologists, but they do not have the intensity of emotion that comes with the issue; their approach is much more clinical."

Ginger moves among the thirty-two bands tracking each horse by age, sex, markings, band stallion and bachelor groups. Working much like birdwatchers with a printed list, we check off those we've seen.

She introduces me to Lakota, a gunmetal-gray stallion who travels with only one mare, a thin bay who ran away from a ranch down below and found her way up to the mountains. I am rooting for the happiness and survival of these little families, and I want Lakota to have more than one fragile domestic mare. I am, of course, already hooked by the heartstrings.

"Come on, we're really close to something special," she says, leading me up the slope past the three small bands to the rim of the mountain where the Crow reservation of Montana spreads out in more than two million acres of mostly trackless miles in all directions. It is, like the horses, undisturbed, unchanged, a prehistoric-looking landscape.

"It's a vision-quest site. The Indians still use it," Ginger explains as we walk to the cliff's edge where a horseshoe of rocks is stacked open to the deadly drop. "It's where young Crow men stand until their spirit animal appears."

I touch the little silver galloping horse I wear on a chain around my neck, purchased at the Billings airport. For a moment I consider hanging it on a twig as an offering in this high and majestic place, the Bighorn River to the right, the clay, sage and violet-streaked desert to the left. Then I decide I will carry this memento with me, along with the images of the silver, dun, bay and black horses it recalls.

It's as dry and hot as the hinges of hell up here in summer. And nothing much can live here in winter, so the horses move constantly to find food, Ginger tells me. They pick their paths down Sykes Ridge or Tillet Ridge to the lowlands for winter, then up the same ridges via ancestral horse trails for the summer.

Through decades of debate, the Bureau of Land Management (BLM), National Park Service and U.S. Forest Service "came to an uneasy and complicated agreement about where the horses can be, whether they should be driven back behind a fence when they come down to forage," she explained.

The issue is heated because cattle ranchers graze (as of 2022) some 2.1 million head cheaply on 251 million acres of Western land, resulting in documented evidence of devastated fragile ecosystems. Ranchers blame wild horses and burros, of which there are an estimated 56,000, and collaborate with the BLM to round up and remove horses by the thousands. Yet there are no wild herds on 87 percent of that land.

Ginger is here seeking the answer to the mystery of where Cloud winters. For five years running, the stallion has disappeared in autumn, only to re-appear for foaling and mating season in the spring. No doubt there are nooks and crannies, springs and forage known only to the generations of wild horses, she says, who have subsisted here for centuries.

That afternoon, we go looking for Cloud, keeping an eye for Opposite, War Bonnet and Raven, the fine-boned black stallion.

Parenting is the job of stallions as well as the mares, she notes, pointing out that a stallion named Plenty Coups formed his first band with orphan foals left on the mountain when their mothers were driven down by the BLM cowboys—a practice that dooms foals left behind to become lunch for bears or mountain lions.

Mountain lions are a factor in the deaths of some of these horses. And some ranchers that bring in the BLM to "manage" them with roundups also reduce the herds. There are other dangers as well. Ginger worries that the unusually high number of dead foals and adult horses in a past year may be due to some virus or a parasite that wild horses had not encountered in their high, dry aerie.

Bears, weather, cattle ranchers and the BLM are threats to the bands, and in addition, there are hazards at this altitude created by the vast open land. Ginger points out a hillside where five horses were struck by lightning.

It is the quintessential West, this harsh horse haven. Some of the limestone formations have been hollowed by rainwater into countless grottoes and caves, some with pictographs. And there is wildlife beyond the mammals: Ginger flaps her arms and a grouse, high above us in the Douglas firs, shoots out and down the slope.

She has herself adopted three Mustangs from the bands: Trace, Flint and Sky. She shows me photos of her great nieces in tie-dye T-shirts riding the horses at her home in Colorado Springs.

Back at the cabin as sunset dims the landscape, Ginger splits firewood outside the cabin with sure swings. A wild horse supporter named Trish is there to keep the fire going and help out, and we restore ourselves over a hot meal of elk, rice and red peppers by a hissing gas lantern and a blaze in the wood stove.

What with Trish's and my purchases at a convenience store and Ginger's supplies, we have brought too much food and far too much wine. I'm relieved when another friend and her husband show up to share some of it. After they leave that night, snow spits through the chinks of the weathered log walls and the wind howls at the warped old roof boards. I thrash all night, chilled even in my mummy bag with my parka thrown over it.

I recall the Donner party, think of grizzlies, of hantavirus, of the chlorine fumes from the bleach Ginger sloshed on the floor to ward it off. I speculate on whether we would open the thick latched door in the morning to trackless snow and not be able to get down the mountain at all.

I also wonder if the car rental company at the Billings airport will discover I had taken their four-by-four in places where no rental four-by-four is permitted to go, 8,000 feet up to the edge of winter into a roadless wild horse preserve.

We rise when Cola whines and clicks across the floor planks; the water in the dog's dish frozen and the fire in the wood stove has gone out.

"When it's too cold to stay in Pen's cabin, let's get the hell off the mountain," says Trish, and she gets no argument from us. We cram our stuff into the Jeep and jounce, jolt and slide down the mountain.

Ginger is one of the world's chief horse documentarians, and her films, books and information are useful to the many people drawn to horses who attempt to protect the wild ones.

Her foremother in the movement to protect wild horses and burros was

Velma Bronn Johnston, aka Wild Horse Annie. Annie's efforts to halt government hunting and killing Mustangs by air and motorized vehicles resulted in a 1959 federal law: President Dwight D. Eisenhower signed the Hunting Wild Horses and Burros on Public Lands Act named in her honor.

But the wild ones weren't and aren't well protected now. And their plight continues to draw other people (largely women) to the cause.

In 2022, after witnessing video footage of a tiny foal suffering a broken leg while being chased by a BLM helicopter, Rep. Dina Titus (D-NV) introduced the Wild Horse and Burro Protection Act (H.R. 6635) to end helicopter roundups once and for all. (The injured foal was shot.)

The American Wild Horse Campaign, led by director Suzanne Roy, is working to prevent the horses from being rounded up at the behest of cattle ranchers. More than 50,000 horses are now in holding pens at an annual taxpayer cost of $60 million. Few are adopted. Many are illicitly shipped to slaughter.

What draws horse lovers to this cause? What keeps us working for the wild ones as well as the tame ones, the imperiled and abused, and especially these free-roaming Mustangs who want nothing more than to be left alone? What motivates the ranchers in this struggle?

It's about more than prioritizing profitable private beef herds, I suspect.

"We try to be fact-based, where the ranches and BLM get schizoid and emotional," Ginger tells me. "There is some fear among them somehow. It's as if the horses somehow are confronting them with a question: 'What's your worst fear, if wildness is allowed to run? What bad things are going to happen to you?'"

Anyone who works this hard, decade after decade, is not infatuated but gripped by something stronger.

We don't just love the wild horses, I surmise. In them we see qualities that thrill us, move us, inspire us. And so we horsegirls try our damnedest to protect them.

CHAPTER 7

All the Fun of War

". . . it's the sport of kings, the image of war without its guilt, and only five-and-twenty percent of its danger."
-Robert S. Surtees, *Handley Cross*

He is elegant, regally tall, slim, and coppery chestnut. He is even better than I expected. I have never ridden a horse like this.

As we brush legs, pick out hooves and wipe down the faces of our mounts, Emily Day tells me that Sea Fighter, my horse for this morning's hunt, had been a European International Stakes winner.

Oh good. Oh dear.

Beneath my new buff breeches, my breakfast churns into an acid whirlpool. That means he's bred like a Ferrari is built: for speed, handling, and power. He goes blindingly fast, fears nothing, leaps mighty crevasses and high walls, and is capable of doing this for hours. He is not just a "blood horse," as Thoroughbred folks call their breed, but a fine specimen of it indeed.

I can't tell her that I have half-faked my way into this event, like writer George Plimpton getting into a boxing ring with Muhammed Ali. I can't confess this to Emily, who is the real thing indeed.

Emily's pedigree is as entwined in the horse world as that of her Thoroughbreds. Matthew Mackay-Smith, her late father, was a pre-eminent veterinarian and columnist for equine magazines. He and her mother, Winkie, used to tear off on 100-mile competitive endurance rides. For fun.

Her grandfather, the late Alexander Mackay-Smith, a kind of Renaissance man of the horse world, was an attorney, writer and editor of *The Chronicle of the Horse* for a quarter century, early promoter of the sport of U.S. eventing (a test of three skills: dressage, cross-country jumping and show jumping) and co-founder of the U.S. Pony Club, the American Association of Equine Artists (AAEA) and the National Sporting Library (NSL). He was also the first importer of Cleveland Bays, an English breed favored by the late Queen Elizabeth herself for driving and hunting. Emily's late grandmother, Joan Dunning, bred some of the most sought-after Welsh and Dartmoor ponies in the show rings of America.

Emily left college to marry an Irish steeplechase rider, Jimmy Day, and went back to school after their two sons grew up. They train and sell horses from their farm in a colonial-era region of Virginia between the almost invisibly small hamlet of Paris and her family farm in even teenier White Post.

None of this shows in the casual way she has invited my friend Lucy and me into her converted dairy barn where we are cleaning bridles and shoveling manure.

I had seen Emily's photo in *The Chronicle of the Horse*, a graceful, slim young woman astride an equally graceful Thoroughbred.

"You need an Irish sport horse or an Irish draft—they're supposed to be the best for hunting," I had told Lucy a year or so previously. She was shopping for a horse to replace Dude, her dear old gimpy Quarter Horse gelding. After reading up on the attributes of many breeds, I wanted to see what I'd never seen—Irish sport horses, Virginia, riding to hounds—and hoped she would buy into it all as well as purchase a horse.

Now, we were in northern Virginia, traveling down lanes hushed by ancient trees and vines, sleepy with a slight Southern edge of menace, history and mystery. On a misty morning above the Shenandoah River a few days before, we watched the members of the Blue Ridge Hunt set off across fields in a scene every bit as picturesque as I had read.

The previous day, Lucy and I had spent the sunny afternoon popping gently over coops, trotting and walking her wide pastures with Emily. Lucy was aboard a big-boned Irish chestnut named Rocky, who had a laid-back attitude and a moose-like head with a white blaze. If she were pleased with him, he would make the thousand-mile journey from Virginia to her own farm in Minnesota.

That was practice.

This was a hunting morning, something radically and wondrously different; something, I was learning, that gives participants a taste of the nerves before a battle.

After a virtually sleepless night, the two of us arrived at Emily's farm snugged into our new duds, prepared to appear as traditional, elegant and upper crust-y as everyone around us. After we mucked, groomed, and saddled, Emily, who does this three times a week or more, simply slipped on her grandmother's ancient thermal undershirt, as perforated as Swiss cheese, then covered it with the traditional white stock tie and black coat.

"Imposter!" I told myself. "You're from a packing-house town. You grew up breathing sausage factory fumes, not the aroma of Virginia ham. These people have been doing this for generations, all the way back to England, Ireland and Prussia, while your grandparents were slopping hogs, gathering eggs and milking Holsteins."

"Karin, I am skeeee-aired!" Lucy whispers to me, her usual jolly face flushed and pale at the same time.

There's no question this kind of riding provides a shot at glamour with an historic flavor. To ride to hounds, tradition decrees there is twill and gabardine, flannel, windowpane, houndstooth and tweed. Boot, bridle and saddle leather are rich and buffed. We may be scuffed, sweaty, scratched and muddy later on, but at the outset, the two of us Midwest horsegirls look proper in an eighteenth-century way. (Think *Outlander* series if you wish—little has changed.)

At the meet, we unload the horses, scoot into the horse trailer one by one for the requisite pee in the floor shavings, then tighten our girths, adjust our stirrups and hoist ourselves onto our saddles from a portable mounting block. This is what it's like when the attendant locks the roller coaster bar down over your lap, I think, and you clack off on the ominous track. There is no turning back.

A couple dozen foxhounds mingle among the horses and joyfully roll in the grass. My hair rises on the nape of my neck, and I feel keenly hungry. I can scent the moist earth, manure, vapors (Brandy? Cognac? Rum?) from someone's pocket flask. The MFH (master of fox hounds) welcomes and introduces us and other guests to three dozen member riders, but I can barely hear her for the blood in my ears. I am alive, more alive than I can remember being.

Then, following each other, Lucy on Rocky, me aboard the terrifyingly fit Sea Fighter (Saint Hubert, god of the hunt, just let me stay on!), trotting behind the master. We are off!

Following the hounds, we crest a hill at a gallop that does not slow on the downward slope, then leap a coop pinched between two oak trees. I rein hard left to avoid crashing over a bank into a brook and sweep back toward the field, as the group of riders is called.

"Oh, that's the one we call Breakneck," says the field master (the rider we follow), an understatement that is amplified by his Virginia accent, as I catch up with him. "We cut half the branches off last year, but somebody is still pretty much always breaking a collarbone or something on it."

I am shaking. I am hooked. I am done for. I am vividly, exquisitely happy. I will never be the same.

We are riding in farm country containing the last vestiges of its colonial-era quiet as it faces the crush of tech worker and executive housing developments billowing out of Fairfax County toward Dulles and Chantilly. We canter across fields and leap walls where young George Washington surveyed. Colonel John Mosby led his troops to battle near here. A few miles away, and a few centuries later, General George Patton did exactly what we are doing, no doubt with much greater dash and complete confidence.

The first time I saw Middleburg, the horsiest town in America, I thought, "I'm home!" The sense of peace, the past, the devotion to horses, caught me in an instant. The feed mill on the main street was fragrant with straw and fifty-pound bags of carrots. There was one stop sign. Ancient maples flamed against white clapboard and brick colonial storefronts where saddles gleamed above window boxes of lavender and rosemary. Petite gardens behind hand-laid stacked stone walls revealed holly, yew and creeping thyme.

First Lady Jackie Kennedy retreated here to ride, which allegedly drove the Secret Service crazy, because they couldn't follow her. Photos of her on horseback with John Jr. and Caroline are still found in the village shops.

At the annual Christmas parade, horses and hounds process down the street past the Red Fox Inn (circa 1728) where President Jack Kennedy and Pierre Salinger held meetings while Jackie rode to hounds.

And now, magnificently mounted, Lucy and I endeavor to keep up, stay on, and look half so cool. The pace is set by the first flight (the group of riders that jumps), mostly locals who have done it since their parents tugged breeches over their diapers and strapped them onto a pony on a lead line.

This morning, hounds sing as they strike a scent, and we gallop, scrambling up and down hillsides times beyond count. I feel like Eliza Doolittle costumed for Ascot but secretly not one of them. At least I'm not Auntie Mame, I tell myself. I can ride: maybe not usually at this level and speed, but I have a chance of staying on. Or will it be paraplegia, quadriplegia, or a simple concussion?

When we pause (called a check) to gather hounds and reconnoiter, the Shenandoah morning mist mingles with the steam off the horses' chests and flanks in the cool air.

Shut up and try to relax, I think. I can shut up, and as time passes, I sort of relax.

Most of all, I worry I am going to humiliate myself in front of some of Virginia's finest horsewomen and men, people who go blithely over three-foot stone walls and wooden coops without breathing hard or mussing their white stock ties. Tying that tie is an art, by the way, and mine looks like Ichabod Crane went at it after a long night of drinking hard cider.

By the fourth jump, Lucy and Rocky are gone out of sight along with Emily, vanished in the thunder of the lead riders. They are so far ahead that the hounds are out of sight, then out of hearing.

I am here, tethered to Sea Fighter by four reins, thanks to a combination of macho and research. This is my equivalent of a midlife crisis—a man would have chosen a BMW convertible and a cocktail waitress and not got his neck broken.

It's not that I haven't jumped this high. I jumped Gabe bareback over three-foot-tall barrels and higher until his early twenties. I had taken lessons, trotting and cantering over poles in an arena on school horses, a controlled situation.

This, however, is not trail riding or lesson riding.

Sea Fighter tries to puzzle me out and accommodate my unspoken wishes—which means we head for a jump and halt, his hooves skidding into the boards. Horses sense ambivalence, and today his rider is conflicted.

"Lean back!" someone yells as we gallop down another steep, muddy bank and clatter into the creek again.

In hunt country, your love of horses follows you literally to the grave: near Delaplane, less than an hour away, I had rambled in an 1840 churchyard with stones inscribed "Respected Horseman" on one flat gravestone and "Equestrian" on another. Dying doing what you love is not a joke here, although judging from the dates, the dearly departed had long since hung up their spurs.

Yet not everybody in hunt country is a horse lover. The previous night, we had feasted on crab cakes at The Ashby Inn in nearby Paris. Later, we sat in the inn's library, Lucy with tawny port, me with ice water, as fire flickered in the old hearth and warmed the fender. John Sherman, owner of the inn with his wife Roma, the head chef and a horsewoman herself, sat with us.

"Every time you ride, it lowers your IQ ten points," John, a fly fisherman and ardent non-rider, told us. "You know why stock ties are long and have a big pin, don't you? They are to bind up your broken arm or shoulder after you crash."

"I wish you hadn't told me that," said Lucy.

Everywhere from Paris to Millwood to Middleburg and beyond, I felt as if I was home at last: gardens brimming with roses, lavender and sage, brooding limestone churches, canopied four-poster beds, harness brasses gleaming in the half-gloom of ancient hearths, dogs and horses invited, discussed and depicted everywhere. And when my waitress who served ham and mashed potatoes at The Coach Stop in Middleburg (where three equestrian newspapers were stacked by the counter) fell into conversation about her three-year-old, it was her Thoroughbred and not a toddler we discussed.

Men ride like crazy here, compared to the rest of my stops, yet not only are many hunt staff and foxhunters female, they are bringing back riding sidesaddle—veil, skirt, and all says Smoky Everhart, a local resident who restores sidesaddles.

"Middleburg is in the middle of ten hunts, and you can get to any of them in twenty minutes," said Everhart, a longtime foxhunter. "And it's coming back more than ever, because there's so much private land here: it's open rolling country, and you can really gallop."

"I love the countryside, and foxhunting is an entree into the inner sanctum of beautiful country," Peter Winants, head of the National Sporting Library in Middleburg, told me. "I love the challenge of making a horse go well in a crowded situation when they are apt to get excited and unruly. Also, I like the people I do this with, they share a bond."

"And they are not the stereotype of rich bastards on horses," Winants added. "My friends and I do our own stable work and make our own horses, there are no grooms making it easy. People work hard for the sport they get, and there's nothing snobbish about it."

Riding fast is another dimension of working hard to those—me, in this case—unused to hunting. Sea Fighter is not the least unruly, he's just unfamiliar to me. So is racing toward fence after fence, and boom! We are over. Buoyant electricity hammers from his hooves to my hips and hands, and my sweaty hair prickles under my helmet. I hear nothing but the faint fine chorus of hounds as his breath comes strong and rhythmic. I'm at a coop (a wooden jump with slanted sides) and we take it long, low and easy and pound on up the hill in fervent eagerness to follow, to see, to smell the leaf-lit red-gold morning.

We sweep through pastures where an old brown barn is slowly dissolving, pass bemused cattle, then head into the woods, horses slipping where the track of limestone becomes mud.

"Lean back!" the field master cries again, and we skid downhill, splash through a creek and slog up the far side, reining in around tight turns, opening up across meadows, hounds barely heard for the wind in our ears, horses enthralled and happy together, ears up and eyes bright.

At some point, an hour or so out, the sunlight falls on the scarlet-coated master on her gelding, cooling his legs in the singing riffles of the creek, hounds arrayed around her, the thong of the old and well-oiled whip with its antler handle coiled in her hand. I realize I am sharing a rare thing, a glimpse of the world the way it looked, sounded, and smelled some two centuries ago.

At another check, the field master passes around her flask of "suntan lotion," and we sip sweet coconut juice and rum in horseback communion, comparing horses, marveling at the bright woods around us.

Other than my personal destruction, I had entered this day with only one real concern: the welfare of the foxes.

In answer to my question, a lady rider tells Lucy and me, "We root for the foxes. We even put out chicken carcasses with de-wormer in them so they don't get mange."

"In all the years I've been hunting, we only caught one once; it was old and probably sick, and it ruined our whole day, everybody felt bad," says another rider, a woman on a bay horse.

On over hills we go. The hounds sometimes announce they scent a fox, but we never view one. At times, we lose the hounds altogether, catching up again by following the horn.

Around three hours out, Lucy and I and other riders head back to the trailer. The horses could go on, but we are satisfied. And we are, frankly, done in.

We dismount, handing over the horses to Emily, and wobble toward the car, our boots slick with dew, horse sweat, creek water, and our own perspiration. We have helmet hair, and we don't care. We feel leggy and lean, hard and happy.

And tired. My legs shake so I can barely walk to the potluck feast set out on a tailgate: cold fried chicken, cookies, chips and salsa, cold salmon and capers and coolers of beer and wine.

"I don't think people who ride outdoors need therapists," says Lucy, whose own career has included becoming a psychotherapist. "They are too busy being happy or working to sit and introspect about their feelings."

We toss down some water and a snack, then retreat over the hills to the Ashby Inn, where we swagger into the dining room in our boots, ignoring the sign that warns, "We have no dress code, although riders with muddy boots and spurs are likely to get very slow service."

John and Roma greet us in the sunroom and pile on thick slices of ham, caviar and sour cream omelets, buttermilk biscuits, white beans with fennel, and shrimp. Roma ladles it on our plates with an unspoken serving of shared knowing of where we have been, what we have seen.

Rosy-faced and joyful with morning, horses and the Shenandoah Valley air, we toast the day, the hunt, the Virginia autumn and ourselves with tulip glasses of champagne.

If we never do another thing in our lives, we have done this.

"We stayed on!" we say, in unison.

CHAPTER 8

Horsegirl Psyche

"I just point out that it feels very much like bliss."
~ **Melissa Holbrook Pierson,**
Dark Horses and Black Beauties: Animals, Women, a Passion

What's in the hearts of horse crazy girls? Do horse-loving women share psychological traits?

Dr. Susan Abraham, MD, dived into my question with the directness of a rider heading a mount at a jump: no swerving, no equivocating, just a fierce, happy, certain force. I should not have been surprised, since she is a skilled rider and trainer and owns half-a-dozen horses.

Abraham was head of adult services at a private psychiatric hospital in Putney, Vermont, where her specialties are personality disorders, post-traumatic stress disorder (PTSD) and eating disorders.

She owns a shifting assortment of horses. Where I tend to hang on to horses for their lifetimes, Abraham prefers to find them, polish them up, then send them on to someone else. For her, horse barns are a bit like bars to an alcoholic, she said.

"I am a horse slut, a horse nympho—I always want new ones," she said. "My friends John and Beth have a resale barn where they go to get horses. I can't go there with them anymore, because I come home with a horse. I like to get them young, train them and sell them. I like letting go. Too many horses, too little time. I like riding anything, but my fancy 'keeper' horse is a Dutch Warmblood for eventing, a jumper with a good attitude."

"Horse passion," said Abraham, turning more serious, "has to do with having a close relationship. Many women who ride have had problematic relationships with their mothers, and certainly many people have that. It has to do with feeling really close to another being and doing something together."

This dovetailed with what my Minnesota trainer and friend Judy had told me about women she knows in horse barns. Judy claimed she could walk down the aisle looking at the horses in her stable and say of their owners, "This person was a druggie, that person is an alcoholic, this person is in recovery, that one came from a really screwed up family, this one is bulimic," and so on, from stall to stall. Horses, it appears, are emotionally necessary and particularly effective for some females. But perhaps no more than the kids who form supportive or escapist communities in theater or their softball or bowling leagues or basketball teams.

So are some of us lost girls, I wondered, motherless in some sense and compensating with a big animal? And yet I know many whole and happy families where mom, dad and daughters (sometimes even sons) all ride.

As Susan Abraham spoke, I felt the furtive thrill I get when I am getting a bright, direct answer to my question and simultaneously learning something about myself, something I would rather not be known by others. I love horses, therefore can wise, incisive people such as Abraham deduce that I had a difficult mother? Whoops!

It's not that simple, perhaps, nor would virtual strangers care.

It had been relatively easy throughout twenty years of daily journalism for me to ask others intimate things about themselves: "How did winning a Pulitzer change your private life?" "What effect did your drug use have on your family?" "Why did you choose to have plastic surgery?" Those sorts of things.

Now, as I put personal questions to horsewomen and ask experts such as Dr. Abraham about horse love, I know some—even many—of the answers apply to me as well.

"In psychology lore, there's a study that looked at ego strength and stress levels of young children who believe 'Mom and I are one,'" Dr. Abraham continued. "Those children who say that to themselves over and over have lower levels of distress. Maybe that study is an urban myth, but that idea seems an important part of this."

"Having a horse is a relationship experience," she continued. "It's a lot like psychotherapy: When it works well, it's a gradual, slow improvement that has to do with increased communication and trust. It's also about power—you can be effective, you can do things, jump over large obstacles, control a big thing."

The passion for horses, she continued, is aligned to the question of where we get our strength, our sense of self as a competent powerful person but also being connected to other people in the world who are good.

"After all," said Dr. Abraham, "we move in herds like horses—unless we're Ted Kaczynski (the so-called Unabomber and recluse)."

We compare horse histories and Dr. Abraham confesses she had gone through a hormonal hiatus and, for a while, collected boys instead of horses.

"Many girls stop riding when they reach puberty," she noted, something I had observed as well, both as a teenager and later on. "I wish I had ridden during my teenage years! But women tend to get horses, or get back to them, when their kids grow up."

I see this everywhere: the girl who keeps her horse or horses all her life may be as common as the girl who swerves off to motherhood for a while and returns when time and money are available again. I had also noted, over decades, a high percentage of women who choose not to have children but always have horses.

She followed that pattern, if not entirely by choice. Her parents wouldn't buy her a horse, but she rode from age eight to twelve at a small, inexpensive stable. When the stable was sold, the other option was "upscale rich barns, but we didn't have much money, so I stopped riding," she said. At twenty-nine, she and her husband moved to Vermont, where they had job offers. Once settled in Putney, her first task was to buy herself a horse.

Good priorities, I thought to myself.

Another reason for the attraction, she mused, is that horses "fit women's operating style. Look at how women function in the workplace and amass power," said Abraham. "Men tend to be singular and dominant and do-it-my-way, women are more consensus builders who do things in a group. Riding goes along with that; when you compete, you compete with another being on your side. Riding is about building trust and increasing communication over time. There's always something in there with you. When it works, it's fabulous."

So much for the theoretical. How had horses played out in her life? Did she fit a pattern I had seen emerging from women of all ages and states? Like significant numbers of those I had spoken with, Abraham has no children.

"A lot of horsewomen don't have children or aren't married—more evidence for the mother theory, for the relationship problem theory," she said, going squarely at the issue again. "To get married and have kids successfully, you have to negotiate intimacy, conflict, and dependency, and if you can't do that, then it's safer not to be married and not to have children."

How about simply more fun and much more freedom, I wondered. What about the patriarchal presumption that it's "natural" or inevitable that all females want mates and children?

She answered my next question before I could phrase it.

"Horses are a way to do that in a controlled, easier, less harmful way," she explained. "If you get pissed off at the horse, you can put him away or sell him or ask a trainer to ride him. If you are pissed off at your husband, that can lead to divorce. If you have trouble with your kids, there is the chance they can go through child protection or adoption. Stakes are much higher and frustrations are much greater with people."

The only frustrations I've had with my horses have been with my own lack of skill at asking for things correctly. When I learned their language and agreed to wait quietly, all went well, beginning with Gabe. He had been my constant through the suitors of my twenties and thirties. Horses, and Gabe in particular, predated and postdated dating. Horses were and are my four-legged compass and men orbited outside of that.

"I continue to prefer horses and dogs to the people who own and train them," Robin, a horsewoman who covered sports first for my own newspaper and later for the *New York Times* told me. "I always was a misanthrope."

While it could be a kind of protective wisdom as well, I think misanthropy can be the refuge of a disappointed romantic. And many of the horse-loving women I have met are not so much misanthropes as introverts or people who have a strong bond that carries them forward and upward emotionally, something especially handy when our own species disappoints or betrays.

I don't think of horses as four-legged Band-Aids or some kind of Prozac that is especially effective for women. Evidence says they are so much more than that. And besides, we are called to them so very early, well before our disappointments: what are they to us?

So I kept asking.

CHAPTER 9

Heart Horse

Everyone has a horse who is special above the others, one that haunts us forever.

~Anna Blake, *Undomesticated Women*

The pale girl hung over the wire fence in the shade watching me dig in the sun. I had expected to be alone, but the girl was there this broiling August day, peering at me from her backyard, and I didn't have the will to shoo her away.

With dirt up to my bare elbows, tears and sweat running down my face, neck and chest, tickling my stomach and into my jeans, I stabbed the shovel and heaved heavy clay out of the ground in the east-sloping hill above the small lake where the great blue herons stalk.

Into the hole went the turquoise and pink Navajo saddle blankets that I was so proud of when I bought them at fifteen. In went my first and only Western saddle, stirrup leathers carefully folded toward the sheepskin underside, the floral-tooled leather blemished with the small gash on the horn where my belt buckle scraped it in speedy dismounts.

On a gray April day four months earlier, I watched a man on a backhoe carve a trench a few feet from where I now dug, then watched as two men dragged into it the white body of my horse. Gabe was buried wrapped in his blue blanket. I didn't want to see how thin he was or the bite and kick marks of the herd that had driven him off to die as horses sometimes will with an old, sick one.

He was wearing his red halter—take it off and have it haunt me? Leave it on and think of him encumbered in horse heaven? I cannot remember now if I left it on or not. I do not have it now, so it must be with him.

Four summer months had done much to hide where he lay.

The grass had rushed across the soil, and there was no depression of the melting body beneath to guide me. So I took a bearing off the fence line, the trees, the light, the slope of the hill, and I dug in my saddle and blankets.

The girl knew what was buried there. I had used her parents' telephone to call the vet who brought the lavender bottles of phenobarbital to speed the dying horse on. I used it to call the neighbor with the tractor and to send word to my old friend, Richard, who had met Gabe when I took him to college with me more than twenty years before.

Now I shoveled in silence and the high summer sizzle of cicadas.

I leaned into the hard hillside with the shovel and sobbed in the sun and heat and deer flies, and flung the dirt back in, not caring that the girl watched and unable to do otherwise anyway. Then I closed the earth, thick with wild grass roots, in a crude mound over what I had buried.

In the last shovel slice, I slipped in a small white pine in its cardboard pot, hoping the whitetail deer, who love the tips of white pine, would not notice this one, at least until it was tall enough to survive.

Gabe was gone, and now every trace of him was buried, too. I denied myself a lock from his mane, a swath of his white tail. No holy relics to make me weep, to worry about losing. Gone was gone: saddle, saddle blankets, bridle, horse and all. And into the earth went my heart. No more horses, I vowed. No more such pain at parting.

"Don't worry, you'll see him again," the girl at the fence said to me. "There's only one heaven."

Women these days often talk or post on social media about their "heart horse." That wasn't a term when I was thirteen and Gabe came into my life. That wasn't yet a term when he left. Now, we recognize our heart horse. I have had one: Gabe.

In the months and years after he was gone, I turned down offers of other horses, including one from Judy, my riding instructor, who was willing to give me a tall young palomino American Saddlebred gelding. I found myself saying thanks, but no.

I felt eviscerated, and if I allow myself to think about it, I still do. Something fundamental is forever gone. I wondered how anything could hurt this much. How are we so attached? How does a loss like this make us vow "Never again! Never!" How much of me had been buried in that pasture?

I could not find the right term: "partner" is too pale, and "soulmate" has vague theological implications. "Daemon," the term in Philip Pullman's *His Dark Materials: The Golden Compass* sounds a bit evil but might be close to accurate. In this fantasy novel, a daemon is the external animal manifestation of a human's inner self. When her daemon is forcefully excised from a child, part of the life force of the child dies. What goes this firmly, this deeply in the heart, blood or nervous system?

What could possibly devastate us when it is lost? I exhaust myself sometimes with my own questing.

What causes us to light up in the presence of horses, of our one special horse, and to darken in their absence? Would a brain scan or MRI show pulses of unique activity? Do some of us carry energy meridians fed by horses?

I told a professor of neuroscience about my quest, and she sent me a paper authored by four scientists and reviewed by several universities. It compared the neurological highs of romantic love to those of substance abuse. She made an assumption (horse lovers experience romantic/addictive love) that narrowed the question and funneled me toward a cliché answer.

An evolutionary biologist I found in *Psychology Today* believes that our passion for horses is a substitute for pair bonding and love of infants.

"With horses, women are practicing the same skills they use to train their boyfriends and children," she wrote. That seems narrow and presumes females who love horses are all straight and inclined to reproduce.

Personally, as a no-pair-bonder-by-choice who never wanted infants, nope. And as for training boyfriends, I've found groundwork utterly fails to be effective.

As I asked scientists about our attraction to equines, they each answered from their own filter: it's sexual, it's a substitute, it's addiction.

I disagree.

For one thing, it starts seemingly at birth or so very young that it appears intrinsic. From nearly every horse-loving female I queried, I heard, "I have the horse gene."

Teasing out a gene seems impossible at the moment, so I look at other effects and other organs for explanation.

My quest is the source of our initial attraction. Before horses become an endorphin factory for us, or an escape vehicle carrying us to freedom and adventure, or something more ineffable as Gabe was to me, what attracts us?

Does anyone think this might be something entirely different? Something not related to mating or mothering? Does anyone see this might be a wholly different love paradigm, largely but not entirely unique to females?

Could it be that some of us, many of us, literally have horse-susceptible hearts? With Gabe, my love and later my grief were pure. It was uncomplicated, not entangled with unresolved issues or negative experiences. When he died, I lay on the ground with my face in his mane for what seemed hours. I knew there would be no relief.

There are clues about our horse love out there in the realm of science, but so far only trickles of answers. Meanwhile, increasing funds, research, and attention are being paid to the effects of horses on humans: riding programs for the disabled, for the autistic, for prisoners, for those suffering depression, for veterans, for troubled youth, for recovering addicts and others are proliferating.

A doctoral dissertation by Elizabeth Dampsey published by The HeartMath Institute on something called heart rate variation (HRV) cited an experiment showing "that the horse's coherent heart rate rhythm influenced the human's heart rate rhythm to oscillate in a similar frequency. Additionally, human participants were instructed to cultivate thoughts and feelings of appreciation, which was shown to be associated with a state of coherence. Eliciting a state of coherence by sending appreciation to the horse resulted in greater amounts of shared oscillation frequencies between the human and horse" (Walters & Baldwin, 2010).

The research is not confined to the United States. In Italy, at the University of Pisa Department of Veterinary Sciences, Paolo Baragli, DVM, PhD, researcher, and Antonio Lanata, PhD, are examining the connection so many horsepeople claim to feel. "Through high-tech research using wearable monitoring systems and advanced algorithms, they've determined that horses and humans tend to align their physiological responses to emotional stimulation" (*The Horse*, Christa Leste-Lasserre, Nov. 2017).

Not all people are attracted, of course: some females are indifferent, frightened or repelled. If our hearts sync up in some way, do we have a cardiac receptivity that others lack?

And could I ever have another heart horse myself?

I had aligned with horses in general from the time I could crawl and for 28 years with Gabe in particular. In his absence, I rode the horses left in his pasture: Quarter Horse geldings named Bill and Dude, a chunky pinto draft cross named Chico and a small, swift and crafty part-Arabian named Sam.

As they grew old and passed on, the man who owned those horses and the pasture I rented assigned me to find him another horse. No conditions, just "something under $1,000." That was his mistake. I was not programmed to seek out an easygoing middle-aged Quarter Horse that all his friends and family could ride.

I scoped out the classified ads and called about an eight-year-old Arabian gelding. The seller—a woman who needed money for college—and I arranged to meet the next day. This was before the internet, so there were no photos.

That night I saw the gray horse—almost white, really—in my dreams. He had distinctive wide-sprung ribs, and I heard myself calling it a pony belly. He faced me, and his huge, gentle dark eyes and his wide ribs made him look like a pregnant mare.

Walking into the indoor arena the next day, I laughed aloud. There, saddled and tied to the rail, was the horse in my dream. His owner untied him and walked him into the arena to the mounting block. I put my feet in the stirrups. I settled into his saddle. He lifted his compact back. He coiled, he moved off my leg. I had only to think and he responded. I could ride this horse with spiderweb for reins, I thought. The seller called him Shadow although his registered name was Sunny Sam. His pedigree showed he was a cousin to my Gabe, a mix of Gainey Arabians including the legendary stallion Ferzon. She tearfully took my check for this Shadow, a shadow of Gabe. And I took him home.

CHAPTER 10

Western Challenge

"I never like my life so well as when I am on horseback. I think of nothing. I'm only strong and happy."

~Gwendolen in *Daniel Deronda*, by George Eliot (aka Mary Ann Evans)

Lynn's grin came at me from the phone.

"Come on out!" she boomed, bringing wide open Nevada into my tiny office. "We have a great time. You're coming with Sue? Terrific woman! Loved having her here. You gotta come! Do you need a horse?"

Say yes and think about it afterwards is my policy on this adventure.

So I say yes to Lynn Lloyd, and yes to the offer of a horse, because I had said yes to a new friend, Sue Slocum.

The previous autumn, Sue had loaned me Josie, her little demon of a Quarter Horse mare, for a drag hunt on land west of Minneapolis. She and her daughter Edee, then eleven, rode in those Saturday morning events, fast, keen and sure of themselves. Edee, brown hair rippling to her shoulder blades, was jockey-sized with arching eyebrows that gave her an expression of quiet astonishment. She seldom spoke and never gave up, whimpered or fell off Skye, her high-headed Lipizzan gelding.

Sue, petite with a thick auburn pageboy, had a reputation for being generous, taking troubled women into her home or housing their horses, and opening her barn to stray dogs. She proved it when she hauled one of her dozen-plus horses to a hunt for me. Without a truck or trailer at that time, I relied on the kindness of other horsepeople, anyone who had one too many horses to ride.

Then one autumn morning post-ride, Sue and I were leaning against her trailer, watching Josie and Sue's gray Thoroughbred, Lennix, nosing hay bags. I was keeping an eye on my six-year-old nephew, Ryder, all freckle-faced smiles, eating a cookie on the back of Daisy, a caramel and white pinto pony Sue had brought to amuse him while we rode.

Our conversation, like those of all people watching horses and children, was fragmented. Minnesota's Senator Paul Wellstone had just died in a plane crash, taking the hope of the Democratic Party with him.

"I was his student at college," she said. "God, I miss him. Josie, quit that!"

"I was there the first year he taught," I said. "I remember him with the loudspeaker and a headband around his Jewish afro—he was a pistol. Move over Josie, dammit! I miss him, too."

"...do the Western Challenge, it's three weeks of riding in various states... Edee, can you watch Ryder?...starting in California and ending in Iowa..." Sue continued. "We can do the California bit."

"Ryder, you need a helmet—c'mere," I urged.

"We could drive out, I'd bring a horse for you," Sue continued. "You'll never meet such terrific women. It's extreme riding, but Josie can do it." Sue kept pitching me. I was flattered and thrilled. And when it comes to horses, I am promiscuous.

The urge to see new territory and the prospect of meeting hard-riding Western women quashed any doubts. If Sue was willing to loan me a horse and tolerate me in close quarters, that was good enough for me.

In late March before dawn, I was out the door heading to Sue's forty acres with a suitcase and a packed cooler. When I pulled into the farmyard, she and Edee were shifting tubs of gear into her three-horse trailer. Josie, Skye and Lennix, their legs in thick protective wraps, were already loaded. Into the truck bed went hay bales and huge water bottles. Into the trailer's tack room went our saddles, bridles, books, bedding, Edee's saxophone, pitchforks, grooming kits, riding coats, helmets and manure scoops. Our three evening gowns swung from a makeshift clothes rack over the feed bin.

"We need them for the ball," Sue had told me. "These people like to party!"

Edee slid onto the bench seat behind us, bags of candy and chips at her feet, seat pockets stuffed with books. Sue slurped the first of many coffees.

"Horses are my therapy," Sue told me as we rolled south and west, crunching pistachios and flicking shells out the truck window. "If I am crouched over while riding, then I'm protecting myself. If I am strong and go at it, then I live that way. If I am open to fixing my riding, then I'm open to changing my life. For me, it takes a mountain of courage to let someone in to fix things, but my riding instructor gets into my shit."

"Horses smell innocence, they treat kids differently," she adds. "Tucker, our dressage horse, often takes a big inhale of Edee, and Skye will do anything for her."

"So what's the difference—puberty?" I ask.

"Kids *ask horses*, and adults *tell horses*," she replies.

As miles and states pass, we swing into a rhythm like a NASCAR pit crew. At gas stations, while the truck sucks down oceans of fuel, we offer the horses water or give them apples for hydration if they won't drink. We check leg wraps, rush to the restroom, heave out rubbish and vroom off.

By afternoon, we are flanked by enormous gray birds feeding in pastures and corn stubble along Nebraska's Platte River. It is peak sandhill crane migration. A half-million cranes and geese swarm the skies and blanket the ground—the largest avian migration in the world.

By sunset, small towns thinned out to a full gas tank apart, and the west wind brought spitting snow. We were headed into a prairie howler. The radio reported five-foot drifts choking the roads in Denver, and all I-80 traffic was ordered to stop at Ogallala, Nebraska. We weren't going to make it anywhere near the B, B and B (bed, breakfast and barn) Sue had reserved in Cheyenne, Wyoming. In the dim cab, I punched the phone as we tunneled on into falling snow and rising wind.

In Ogallala, I reached a vet clinic that would house the horses. We unloaded them on the dirt track of the nearby fairgrounds. Skye, Lennix and Josie were eager to rip and roll after hours in the trailer. For whatever alpha mare reason, Josie makes a point of snorting on me when I pass her head and farting when I pass her rear. And I haven't even ridden her or told Josie what to do—yet.

"Geez, your horse doesn't respect me at all, Edee," I say as Edee giggles. "I swear she saves it all up."

After we tuck the horses into a pen at the clinic, we climb onto the fence at the cattle auction yard opposite to watch cowboys sell cows to other cowboys. The stockyard handler's horse pivots, wheels and scurries, opening and closing gates, hustling black Angus into the ring and out, moving as if oiled.

"You guys are more interesting than I thought you'd be," Edee says as we crawl, dead tired, to our motel.

At dawn I look out to see semis parked nose-to-tail along the freeway shoulder. Ogallala has swelled into a sea of idling engines, their drivers watching The Weather Channel. Edee flops on the bed playing Equistar, a video game that simulates a cross-country jumping course.

I walk down the bleak corridor and find Sue in the motel hot tub with a three-hundred-pound trucker. I do not join them.

"I'm practically blind, but I won't wear glasses," says Dan from South Carolina, blinking pale eyelashes. Amid the bubbles, Dan is wearing shorts and, I notice gratefully, a tank top.

"That's got to be dangerous for driving—why don't you have Lasik?" I ask.

"Cause I like contact lenses: you can get 'em with shamrocks and tiger eyes and things," Dan reveals. "I like to wear 'em in bars."

I leave Sue to simmer while I pick through a brochure rack in the lobby. Ogallala boasts the "second-largest Quarter Horse ranch in North America" which means in the world. I survey the stranded truckers chewing stale doughnuts and dial the Figure 4 Ranch.

"Hi, we're Minnesota riders stuck in Ogallala because of the snow, and we heard about your ranch," I ask, hopefully. "Could we take a tour?"

"I'm sorry, the ranch is closed to tours right now. Those only happen in summer," a woman with a mild Western twang tells me.

I weigh the entertainments left to us and try again.

"Well, let's start over: Hi, I'm a journalist, and I write for publications including the *AQHA Journal*. Could I come up and visit?"

An hour later, we pass through wrought iron gates into the wide, treeless beauty of the Figure 4 Ranch, a half-dozen low barns and ranch buildings with porches. In the banquet hall, where taxidermied Longhorns preside, a buffet lunch is laid out. Owner Craig Haythorn, a towering strawberry blond with a handlebar mustache, greets us with "You eaten yet?" as sunburnt ranch hands in chaps and spurs jingle in out of the cool morning and remove their cowboy hats to reveal fish-belly-white foreheads. Edee, Sue and I pile our blue-and-white enamelware with hot chicken fingers, gravy and green beans.

Craig spends the rest of the day driving us from vast pasture to vaster pasture viewing weanlings and mares, stallions who race our truck, and Belgian draft horses (used to haul feed) dozing in the winter sun.

It is a woman-less landscape except for us; Edee silent but intent, while Sue and I ask questions. Forgetting for a moment Western protocol about never asking a man the size of his spread, I do.

"It's 65 miles from north to south, 90,000 acres," says Craig, taking no offense. He is the third generation of an English immigrant family. "My grandfather wanted to marry my grandmother, but they were only fourteen, so he stowed away on a boat and ended up in Texas droving cattle to Ogallala."

At dinner, down the mountain, Sue and I swig beer and chew rubbery Rocky Mountain oysters (calves' testicles) as, through the café window, I contemplate our truck's bumper sticker, which declares "Geld 'Em!"

"Highway crews are setting off avalanches between Cheyenne and Laramie to clear the passes—we sure can't go that way," Sue notes. "Denver is closed to the south. We're already missing the first day, and I'm getting fat and cranky! So are the horses. They're going to lose condition, too."

We agree to circle north to Casper, Wyoming—an additional 250 miles, but it will keep us moving toward Lynn's ranch. At dawn, with fresh hay and water, we shoot out of Ogallala listening to Ernest Hemingway's *True at First Light* on the radio. The plains of Africa seem mirrored by the plains around us: pale gold pronghorns, prairie dogs standing sentinel, the occasional ostrich, emu or Longhorn cattle ranches. When Hemingway shoots his old friend, a gelding, for bear and eagle bait, I weep silently.

Hours later, I step out of the truck and pinch a sprig of sagebrush, inhaling the plum, tan, smoky green terrain. Edee, too modest to pee in several hundred thousand uninhabited acres, scoots into the trailer to squat in the shavings alongside her mare. Scanning the exuberant sweep of bison-colored hills, switchbacks into galloping country and vast valleys between ancient volcanoes the color of autumn grass, I think: I could go on forever.

"This is where I belong," Sue says, as if she'd heard me.

Sue had graduated high school in Billings, Montana, then started trading futures at nineteen during summers while in college. After college, she became a commodities trader ("pork bellies—really") in Manhattan, taking the subway with Edee on her back, a purse, a diaper bag and a briefcase. Now, because of horses, she abides in an opposite universe.

We drop down The Sisters, steep switchbacks descending toward Salt Lake City, Sue dialing the trailer brakes tighter with her left hand while steering with her right. How the hell did pioneers ever get down this mountain with horses and wagons and no roads, I wonder.

On to Elko we roll as I read the billboards: "Home of Cowboy Poetry. They Only Write What Their Horses Tell 'em" and then Battle, Utah, "The Armpit of America According to the Washington Post, Make Us Your Pit Stop."

We roll through a boiled landscape. Steam rises from hot springs, dust devils whirl and vanish, sere ridges split open to stripes of salmon rock. Vernis veins of snow cascade down organ pipes and goblins. Tumbleweeds mash against the highway fence. It is a Jurassic veldt, a landscape to evoke words from my childhood: Gila monster, Comanches, conestoga, alkali.

After more than 2,000 miles, we pull into Lynn's Red Rock Ranch at the base of The Pinnacles, a jaw of snaggly rock rising up behind her stable. Dogs bark, tractors purr and horses whinny. Cups of wine await riders coming into the yard from the day's trail ride or training on the jump course.

Lynn walks with what can only be called a swagger, accentuated by a well-fitting traditional scarlet hunt coat. Her front teeth gap, and her brown eyes are fired by energy and loud, braying laughs. Her riding boots are set off with hound head spurs custom made for her as a master of fox hounds.

Wherever Lynn walks, she does so in a swirl of dogs: pugs Kieffer, Lynnlee and Chata; Boris the borzoi; Prowler, an Akita; a sheepdog named Chloe; and Sticky, a terrier-coyote who solemnly licks my hands. Here she is, I thought, an androgynous Western Diana, goddess of the cowboy hunt.

Lynn's following of house and barn dogs is a fraction of her pack. In her hound runs, where the Red Rock working and breeding pack of 135 hounds are housed, there are gnawed horse femurs. Lynn feeds flesh, nothing goes to waste.

We bunk at her friend Terry's ranch house nearby. Bunk, literally: we are displacing Terry's sons Marcus and Leo, legacy of Terry's onetime marriage to an Austrian ski instructor. They are lean and leggy blonds who run the dude trail ride business with Terry and work as part-time ski instructors. With full lips, faded jeans, and Western guy swagger, they could be Brad Pitt's brothers.

A blind and affable St. Bernard named Candor flops on an old mattress on the porch. The house pets include Smudge, a "chainsaw dog," Terry explains. "She goes from nothing to RRRRRRRR," and Max, a Queensland blue heeler. There are assorted genial striped gray cats, one laying down a fresh layer of dander and hair on my pillow, one curled up in my suitcase, another on the toilet seat.

We lean against the kitchen counters and suck down bottles of Mexican beer with limes while something that smells like chili simmers on the stove.

"I'll just put this skillet on the floor for the pre-wash cycle," Terry says, plunking one pot down for Smudge and Max. And we talk horses.

"Horses are so emotionally intelligent that they feel your fear, tension—they have to be so sharpened to be able to survive," Sue theorizes as we ponder how horses and women intersect.

"Owning a horse is like getting married first and then dating," Terry observes, and I agree. We also agree horse craziness is there at birth.

"I was only two or three when my parents started taking me to a pony ride, and at nine they got me an old horse," Terry says. "I kept her in a little ranch up in the hills behind Santa Barbara. Every year now, I put 10,000 people (the aforementioned dudes) on horseback, tell them we humans are predators, and horses are prey animals, and explain that prey animals react differently. When horses see anything different, they're outta there, because the last one gets eaten. Horses want to scoot, and people want to scream; it's really important to sit tight and stay quiet around horses. If you are aware of that, you can have a safer, fun ride. Women and girls are usually quieter and do what they are told better."

Lynn gives us a tour of her kennels, clean sheds with box stalls where hounds are grouped by ages. They are frantically happy to see us, and there are hound kisses and slurps all around, bright eyes and wagging tails (what hunting parlance calls "sterns"). Lynn pours kibble and gloppy fat into long troughs, and the hounds gobble, shoulder to shoulder, ears a-flop in dinner. The aroma of burgers and fries rises around us.

"I get this stuff free from a friend who owns a saloon in Virginia City," she says. "Fat makes them shine and gives 'em energy."

Looking through the kennel doors, I spot another course of dinner: horse hooves and leg bones. They are well-shod hooves, too. It's a charnel yard out here in the hound run.

"Lynn feeds flesh, people bring old or dead horses and cattle here," Sue had warned me on several occasions. At least Ethel is not here, not today.

Next morning, saddled up at dawn, fifty or sixty of us fan out behind Lynn and her pack of hounds, trotting up the mountainside in light rain. In the hush at the mountaintop we halt to watch a rainbow rise, shimmer, arc, and touch the earth below us. Two Mustangs at a water tank on the valley floor eye us as riders pry cameras out of their pockets. I don't bother; nothing could capture this.

We move on in an explosion of hooves and dirt. Edee and Skye vanish on the slope below me, and Sue plunges after them, zigzagging on Lennix. I follow, teeth jiggling in concussion as Josie rips along, popping over and around bitter brush and waist-high sage that tear at our boots. The mare won't whoa or slow; she is determined to catch up with her herd even if it means a breakneck run down an unknown hillside.

By day's end, we have been a good twenty-five miles up and down the mountain. Riding in Lynn's wake, we moved so fast I never had time to reach back and unwrap the chocolate bars from my saddle pack, and I am famished. I walk the last three miles on foot leading Josie, her silver coat pinkish brown with dust. She halts and looks at me incredulously.

"Surely we're done now," she seems to say. "You will fetch the trailer and water now, right?"

"Lynn doesn't come in 'til the last man dies," another exhausted walker tells me as we limp home to dinner.

"Didja have fun, honey?" Lynn caws at me, wrapping an arm around my shoulders, and we fall on the ham, fried chicken, pasta and fruit salad.

"Now, about horses and women," I begin.

"I believe horses have been a part of all my lives," Lynn tells me.

Our hard-riding, charismatic leader of the pack tells me she is reincarnated. No doubt General George Patton, also a foxhunter and a believer in previous lives, would resonate with her.

"I was a woman warrior on horseback during the Roman empire. Later I was killed at the battle of Little Big Horn; I was just an ordinary guy with a wife and two children, shot dead. Now I no longer have to kill people, but when I put on a gun or a hat, it does feel comfortable. There is something to that."

"How do you know that?" I ask. I was charmed by Lynn, and when I'm charmed I slip into the charmer's reality, yes-ing and uh-huh-ing and nodding them on. As a journalist, however, I need to prod a bit.

"It comes from dreams, from the fact energy can't go away," says Lynn. "I also have been regressed into my past lives by two psychics—a guy in Pennsylvania and then a woman out here. She came up with the exact same stories he had told me twenty-five years earlier. I was always around horses in my past lives and mostly in the military."

In her current lifetime, teenaged Lynn traveled to Buckinghamshire, England, where she earned certification from the highly rigorous British Horse Society Association (BHSA). She then worked as a stable groom, driving a lorry for a woman who rode to hounds. She was 18, making about $15 a week.

Back in America at twenty-three, with $1,200 in her jeans, she took her dog, Puddles, one change of clothes, a bedroll and a three-pound tent and rode from Pennsylvania to San Diego, California, over seven months. Her intended transcontinental mount, a Thoroughbred gelding, died under her in a steeplechase five days before she planned to leave. A friend gave her a 19-year-old gelding that got as far as Ohio where "he got depressed and quit," she said. "Then I got Bojangles, an Anglo-Arab, and finished on him. He ran away with me for the first hundred miles. I just said, 'Run all you want, boy, just keep heading West.'"

Out of that came her book *Seven Sets of Horseshoes: An American Journey.* And Lynn downplays the ride.

"I'm only the hundred millionth person to do it," she says. "That trip was my education with myself, meeting people, and having to deal with situations."

By this time, after a full day of riding, I am itchy and stiffening up and craving a shower, but her story holds me.

Riding, she tells me, is about being alive in the moment.

"A woman once told me, 'When I went hunting with you, I forgot about my husband, children and bank account.' That's true."

"The other thing about horses is nature," she says. "Horses bring us back to that; our systems still need that. They need farming, the ground. We need to touch the earth, not concrete. People talk about redneck cowboys or ranchers, but I have found ranchers and cowboys to be the most accepting of people of diversity. You learn that because of nature, which is nothing but diversity."

Running up and down mountains is her natural habitat. And over the days with Lynn, I saw her infuse that confidence in the riders with her.

"No, there isn't fear," she said, streaming out cigarette smoke. "I haven't had any major accidents, but I respect others and understand their fear. I have been doing horses all my life. I used to ride big jumpers back East. Now I look at a four-and-a-half foot fence and go 'Oh shit!' Age isn't it. Big-time riders come here to look at horses, they say to me, 'I'm not going cross country here, Lynn!' Doing anything just makes you braver as you accomplish goals."

But Lynn does have fears, I find, and we share them: fear of not being wild, free and frequently with horses.

"Put me in a city, and I'd become a very bad person," she said. "I grew up way out in the country in Pennsylvania. When I was six, I went with my parents into Philadelphia, where there are rowhouses, and all of the sudden I was overcome with fear—I'm talking fear!—that I would have to marry somebody and live in a rowhouse. I've never forgotten that."

As commander-in-chief of her bustling ranch now, Lynn's philosophy attracts all kinds of riders. And when it comes to working for her, more women apply to do the chores of cleaning, tacking and riding horses.

"I wish I had more women," she tells me, unabashedly. "I keep a man to do irrigating and fixing machinery, but if I could, I'd have all women; they are easier to get along with. With men you have to go around their ego all the time. They have to think everything is their idea. Women are easier to direct, instead of getting all defensive. Women by nature are more nurturing, too. It's been proven that if you have an all-women staff at a dairy farm, milk production goes up. Cows respond because women are more gentle on teats."

If it's nurturing, I think, then it's nurturing with a strong Spartan streak: Lynn sends her pregnant bitches to whelp (deliver) at friends' houses, where the pups mature for ten weeks. At least the hardy ones do.

"When I send a hound out, I tell them do not try to save any puppy, do not call the vet on anything. Let nature save the strong ones," Lynn tells me. "The bitch will push a weak puppy out. It does not do well in our situation to save weak ones; it draws the health of the pack down. When I have intervened and saved puppies, I kicked myself later, because I lose them at some point. What lives, lives. The bitch determines, she and nature. If the heart takes over—we've gotta save the poor puppy—well, you can do that with house dogs, but not with a pack of hounds where health really matters."

I ask her about a dead hound we'd found in a dry wash that day. In other packs I know, hounds too old to keep up are retired to homes or live out their days at the kennel. Lynn takes them out with the pack, and if they don't make it home, they don't.

"Wouldn't they rather die doing what they love?" she says.

Terry and Lynn are opposites in some ways, yet they both represent what I'm beginning to see as two general types of horsewomen: Terry is the shy, misanthropic introvert: quiet, lonely, rescuing and healed in the comfort of horses.

Lynn, with her backslapping energy, her deal-making charm, her lack of sentimentality, her non-stop the-world-is-a-party forcefield welcomes you in. It welcomed me in, even if I wanted to skitter off into a corner and watch.

Out by the barn, I watch Terry in the paddock. Someone had vaulted into the pen and tried to catch an unhandled bay colt. Now he was racing around in desperation, rearing and headed for the metal five-rail gate.

Wordlessly, Terry stood motionless as the rest of the crew cleared out. Within minutes, the colt was following her docilely at the end of a lead rope.

"Usually, people tell you that emotional equals stupid," Terry tells me. "I've always done better with animals than people. A lot of people go into a crowd and right up to somebody and talk to them and take command of situations at cocktails or business meetings. I was an only child, so I stand there and see what's gonna happen. That's the proper way to go into a group of horses, too. Modern society tells us not to be like horses. You're supposed to go out and challenge the world, but I react to things."

It's been a long, lovely, uplifting day. Now I find Terry's boys are lounging in their room—our room—sprawled out watching *The Bourne Identity*. Sue is so tired she squeezes into the bottom bunk and goes to sleep while the cinematic firearms blaze. I am desperate for rest, but see I'm not likely to get it here. (Does B, B and B also mean bunkbed and big blond boy?) So I fill my pockets with carrots, filch a handful of bran and horse pellets from the barn and walk through the rich dark to feed Ethel. Ethel, an old white donkey, was half blind, her hooves twisted with founder and thin with neglect when Terry took her home.

"I found her tied out by the hound pen," Terry had told me. "Lynn was going to shoot her and feed her to the hounds."

Ethel hee-haws gently at me as I massage her skinny spine and neck and leans so hard into me that she stumbles. In starry silence, I recharge my introvert batteries for an hour or more with the old donkey.

We ride out each day at dawn and return at twilight to the muted percussion of prairie chickens. There are no humans except riders, and few roads, yet in the middle of miles of sagebrush, an enraged man pops up and yells unintelligibly at us. Behind him, we notice a new modern home under construction.

Lynn's neighbor, a rider named Bodie, says "Now there's a neighbor I have to shoot. I can, too. I live right up there; I can get him from my window."

As the challenge week comes to an end, I take stock of my injuries: a bruise between the eyes from a blanket buckle caught by the wind as I struggled to bundle up a chilled Josie; a tender spot on the top of my head where I scrambled under the gooseneck to reach for water in the truck bed; bruises up and down my legs from stirrups and stairs and staggering into bedframes with weariness. The worst are my lips: caramelized by the sun and altitude, they are split, blistered and swollen. Merit badges, I think, from constant freedom lived in the open air, continuous hard riding and living in a community of happy horses, hounds and (mostly) women.

On the day we leave for home, Lynn gives Edee two hound puppies, Lazatich and E-Mail, who leap into the trailer tack room with her.

At her kitchen door we say goodbye, and I take a last chance to find out more about her, about us.

"What is it about women and horses, Lynn?"

"Women have that nurturing thing," she said, and she pulls shy Edee and Sue and then me into a firm, warm hug.

Yes, of course, but what else: There's much more, I insist.

"Horses give us a tremendous amount of independence—that's the biggest thing. We get on 'em and we're totally free of everything."

As we turn the truck down the dirt drive out of her ranch, Lynn waves from the deck: "Yeeeeeha! Have fun!"

CHAPTER 11

Lady Drivers

"I love driving a four, it gives you an adrenalin uplift. My thing is God take me now! I feel like I'm in heaven."

~Mary Ruth Marks,
Champion sport pony driver

He flailed the lead rope at them as they came zinging out of the door, but the wasps stung the stable manager right between the eyes anyway.

"S...t!" he yelled, trying to muffle his curses in front of his boss, Gloria Austin, and me, her guest.

Behind the bars of the stall, a huge gray gelding danced, wild-eyed. He was anxious enough in his new home after a trip from Europe that took a good week, including quarantine in Miami. Now, seconds after descending from the horse van, he was spooked by wasps, strangers, and a leaping, swatting, cursing human.

Gloria, the picture of a Southern lady in a beige floral summer dress, straw sun hat and loafers, moved calmly into the stall, snapped a lead rope to the halter of the big horse and led him around the corner into a wasp-free stall. Then, one by one, she led out of the van the rest of her six new Kladrubers, driving horses from Czechoslovakia.

I note her hands are plain, she wears no nail polish or rings, and the left index nail is purple—smashed on a carriage driving trip in Europe, she tells me. There will be no smashing today, as the geldings all settle down to munch hay.

Here at Continental Acres, Gloria's 380-acre farm in Weirsdale, Florida, I will be taking driving lessons, and learning something more about the horsegirl phenomenon from one of the most accomplished horsegirls in the world. Gloria is among the tiny cadre who have revived coaching: coach as in royal procession, as in Cinderella, as in pumpkin and mice turned into carriage and milk-white horses.

Women have been passengers since wheels were put under wagons. Sometimes, they are the decorative centerpiece in state events—think Prince Charles and Princess Diana's wedding, the Queen's Jubilee or the bridal processions of numerous others. Very few women, however, drive four or six spirited horses put to heavy, ornate coaches.

I began driving as a kid, when my sister and I contrived a harness out of baling twine and clothesline and skidded around on a toboggan behind our pinto pony, Molly. As a seasoned recreational driver, I've driven vis à vis carriages, rubber-tired carts, wagonettes, sleighs, and bobsleds. But I'm self-taught, and that means largely ignorant of correct ways of handling a vehicle, whip and reins. Before I move up to a pair (two horses), I hope to scour away bad habits: Gloria is one of the few experts in this sport who offers drivers' training.

Competitive coach driving has for centuries been the exclusive territory of wealthy men. One of the men at the pinnacle is the late HRH Prince Philip. Another is Chester Webster, heir to the Campbell's Soup fortune. "Lady drivers" in the competitive arena include Misdee Wrigley-Miller, the chewing gum heiress, and Anne Wakefield Leck, a banking heiress.

Gloria achieved her farm, her skills and her horses the hard way.

As a divorced mom, she raised two children, one of them disabled, while she built up a New York franchise of her Paychex Inc. corporation. Her territory was neighborhoods so tough that she sometimes took a taxi from the door of a client's building to her car one block away.

"I could write a book about doing business as a single woman in the toughest city on earth, the body language, the tricks of conversation, how to get attention and respect, accomplish a goal, and leave in a short time," she told me.

First, however, we go for a drive, a drive in the old, original sense of the word. Beneath her trademark broad-brimmed hat, Gloria has short blond hair and direct, pale blue eyes radiating a kind of steady intelligence and calm energy. Her horses pay attention, and I find myself paying close attention, too.

In the breezy alleyway of her main stable, grooms have harnessed and hooked four Friesians to a coach. A Dutch breed, the curvaceous black horses are distinguished by high heads and luxuriant manes, tails, and leg feathers: the lighter pair, Diewe and Goffe, are the leaders, while Fred and Marten are the wheelers, the heavier-built horses whose buttocks take the vehicle's weight, especially downhill. Gloria's team includes a tall man with a boxer's nose, head trainer Jean-Paul Gautier from the French National Stud in Normandy. Up behind us in the groom's seat is a slim young woman with a white-blond braid hanging down her back: Melissa Warner, a former French teacher, now Gloria's equine manager.

Gloria gathers her flowered skirt, climbs up on the seat (called a box), adjusts the lines and whip, and I clamber up on her left.

Gloria manipulates a delicate whip in her right hand while her left hand holds four long reins. In lieu of a rider's seat and legs, the red silk lash of the whip can reach the shoulders and rumps of the horses. It's a tickle or a tap, not a sting, by the way. Coach passengers, for the most part, sit on bank seats atop the coach, while grooms sit in the seat to the rear, the better to hop down and "head" (hold) the horses at a stop.

"Horses are my passion, my will to live," she tells me, "and it's passion that keeps us vibrant as we age, whether it's tennis or books or bowling or collecting cars. I love to play golf. I used to play softball three times a week, but I have to choose one endeavor. If I get injured, it's serious for my driving. And I have to pursue and practice my craft, keep that muscle memory good enough to enjoy it."

When Paychex was first evolving, Gloria split her time between a home outside Rochester, New York, and her ranch home in central Florida. Later, she moved away from winter forever in order to drive horses year round.

"As mortality comes closer, you don't put things off, it's a race," she tells me, as I admire her steady hands and her deft use of the bow top whip. "I try for balance between time with my partner, my children and grandchildren, my love for horses, and my finances, which are mostly to support and enjoy horses."

"I admit the horses get most of the attention," she adds, and I am not the least surprised.

"My problem is focus and details," Gloria confides. "I see the big picture, the whole world, and driving demands intense focus, more focus than riding. You have to watch continually, to counteract fear and keep things in balance."

At a brisk trot, we roll through her ranch amid lawns dotted with sculptures of herons, sandhill cranes, deer, cougar and fox set among sago palm and azaleas. Her shining geldings listen to her, flicking their ears back and forward as they turn corners, swoop up gentle paths and pass plashing fountains.

White foam drips from their thighs and bellies when she at last threads the team under a colonnaded breezeway and back into the stable. Central Florida summers are so oppressive that her horses receive a ration of rock salt to prevent dehydration, and they are showered after even a short drive.

Under shady live oaks, we walk to visit her herd of "about thirty." In addition to Friesians, Gloria has Selle Français warmbloods with their distinctive Roman noses, a pinto National Show Horse (Arabian crossed with Saddlebred), miniature horses, and Morgan–Friesian crosses that she uses in giving lessons.

As I pass the dozens of gleaming residents of Gloria's realm, I think of that decorative barn sign: "Horses Are Like Potato Chips—Nobody Can Have Just One." In particular, I admire the thick cannon bones, strapping forearms, and substantial hooves of the Kladrubers; leggy, ram-headed grays, a western Czechoslovakian breed established in the early 18th century to pull imperial carriages.

Most Americans know the Budweiser Clydesdales by sight, and although these are something far more rare, they share that presence and what horse people call "substance." They are still used by such royal figures as the Queen of Denmark on special occasions. They arrived replete with substantial red-leather-covered passports and elegant, musical, European names such as Favory Parma XI and Rudolfa Eroica. They are part hot-blooded Arabian and part cold-blooded draft horse—a blend called "warmbloods" in the horse world.

"With driving horses, you want big feet and legs and a light body," Gloria explains.

In addition to her numerous equines, she collects horse-drawn vehicles and driving paraphernalia: she opens the door into a vast cool room, where we pass carts, wagons, sporting vehicles, and gear, including an 18th-century Italian postillion harness replete with badger fur collar, bells and tassels, and a stage coach straight out of the Roy Rogers, Gene Autry and Hopalong Cassidy movies of my childhood.

Gloria doesn't just compete, she knows the arcana of driving, its gear and garments: the number of buttons on a coachman's coat versus a groom's coat, for example, and how an owner drives wearing a gray top hat and the harness has chain traces, while a groom wears a black top hat and uses leather traces.

Not only class status but the gender of the driver was reflected in the design of some horse-drawn vehicles.

"Some Victorian-era vehicles had a modesty panel on the dash, elevating it so the lady driving would not have a view of a horse's rump," she tells me.

Her own passion for horses started with a pony on the family farm near Corning, New York. Her father was a horseman who left school at 15 to tend the horse teams used by road building crews.

"When I was a kid and went out on my pony, my parents never asked me where I was going, who I was with, or when I'd be back," she recalls. "I went down the road and through creeks and didn't have to tell them anything. I had my horse with me, and they let me know that meant I was safe."

Like many horsegirls, she took a break from horses for school, career, and children.

"When I was twenty, I sold my Paso Fino to pay for college books," she explained. She studied public administration and attained a master's degree. "I spent twenty years without horses, then on my forty-something birthday I wanted to ride again. At the Royal Agricultural Winter Fair in Toronto, I had seen old geezers on coaches, so old they looked like they would fall off; they couldn't ride anymore, but they could still drive. I knew my knees would age, and I thought why not drive? So I bought a pony with a runabout and a sleigh, and then I bought a paint driving horse.

And like all of us, she cannot, will not, stop.

"At forty-five, I said I'd buy my last horse, and I got a palomino to ride and drive," she said. "Since then, I've owned some two hundred horses."

What is it about females in our madness for horses, I ask her.

Gloria suggests that horses act for women and girls as an equalizer between genders.

"In most cultures, women don't have political, economic or physical power," Gloria offers. "Maybe horses give us power over something much bigger and a way into the world, a path to venture into it. I always envied the role of men, who are encouraged with physical power and freedom, while we as women are literally and psychologically restricted."

"That's why I travel with horses, it is the way to be okay out in the world."

"Horses operate on instinct; women are bound up in relationships and feedback and interaction. Whether innate or trained, we get along better with animals. We read more than the intellectual in them. We look at a horse and ask, 'Is he unhappy, how is he feeling today?'"

"We are used to operating that way in the world, not by backslapping. If you are really into horses, your senses are stronger, and in driving your senses have to be even more tuned in—you have to be more sensual but maybe use less intelligence."

On the grounds of Continental Acres, Gloria has put me up in one of her guest cottages with a kitchen, living room, spotless bath, and an attached six-stall stable. That night, I slip out of bed in my white cotton nightgown and dance barefoot down the airy aisle in the dark, wishing there were horses—my horses—in the silent stalls.

The next morning, the first day of lessons, I meet my school horse, a small, chocolate-brown Morgan cross, obviously the slowest and most trouble-free of her herd. With Gloria seated in the cart beside me, we walk and trot gently and enjoy the paths through her property. She shows me how to bridge my reins, the correct angle to hold the whip, the right pressure on the lines to ask for turns.

On the second day, I am promoted to a brisker steed for practice on the trails, and on the third day, we enter a groomed dressage ring. There, she exhorts me to guide him at what I think is a pretty speedy trot along the rail, skimming millimeters away from orange cones and bending closely into corners.

"Tap, tap, tap," she tells me, and I touch the whip to his side to cue him while guiding him with the reins, laughing in anxious delight, Gloria chuckling. Power, lightness, response, speed—these are terms for sports cars, but I find them true of this surefooted, flexible little guy in front of me as well.

She teaches me the traditional vocal cue for slow and whoa, a trilling "pr-rrrrrrrrr!" used mostly by European drivers.

After lessons, over iced tea and seafood salad at a nearby golf course, we talk horses, their allure, their effect on women.

"Horsewomen are more masculine in some ways," Gloria says. "It's in how they move in the world, they are freer, and in how their body moves."

Gender and prohibitions against women drivers played a role in Gloria's competitive drive.

"The New York Coaching Club and British Coaching Club didn't admit women, so in 1983, women started their own, expansively and inclusively one-upping the men by naming it The World Coaching Club," Gloria says. "Founders Cynthia Haydon, the late Gay Robinson and Anne Leck started it as a lark, but they were—and we are—serious."

At Walnut Hill, a farm outside Pittsford, New York, she won the national pair-driving championships with her Morgan–Friesians in 1994 and '95.

"It was pure joy to drive on roads where my ancestors did," she recalls. "So I had won a North American championship and thought, what next? I went from driving pairs to driving four-in-hand."

At the Royal Agricultural Winter Fair in Toronto, driving Goffe, Diewe, Gaika, and David, she won both the 1998 North American Coach and the Four-in-Hand Championships with her Healy Park Drag, a gorgeous big Cadillac of a coach.

"I don't really think about competing, just about not embarrassing myself," she says, to my surprise. "There was Sir John Richards driving next to me, and I thought, well, the men won't let me in the club, but I can drive with them."

Former chair of the British Driving Society, Sir Richards competed for Great Britain, twice won the Royal Windsor Horse Show, and was publisher of Prince Philip's, Duke of Edinburgh, book on carriage driving.

Next, she took on driving in Europe, and in 1999 Gloria became the first American since Alfred Vanderbilt to take her team to competition in England. She was the only lady driver among sixteen entries at Windsor. Then it was across the English Channel to compete in France, where there were no other women in the four-in-hand class in Cuts, northeast of Paris, either.

"Women were driving in competition but only ponies," she says. Ponies are the go-karts of the horse world, and their greater ease of harnessing and handling makes them appealing to smaller and less bold drivers.

In the boom years before the Great Depression, driving in Europe was fashionable among well-to-do Americans, she notes, and "most of all they went to study four-in-hand with Edwin Howlett, to drive the streets of Paris. Alfred Vanderbilt, who drove often in England, later perished on the *Lusitania* with sixty horses, his coaches and staff and almost a thousand other passengers."

"It bothers me that some people treat horses like pets," Gloria says, bringing up behavior of which more women than men are guilty. "They can hurt you, so I insist on perfect behavior. I tend not to present a horse unless they do in public what I ask of them in private."

In driving, especially, manners matter. Runaways are so very much worse than in riding—messier, more protracted, traumatic for the horse as well as driver.

I've only had two driving runaways—well, three, come to think of it. No, four, beginning with a tire blowing on our new red cart the first time out with

Molly. She bolted in panic, and Dad, my sister Gayle, and I spilled into a ditch inches from the barbed-wire fence. It was the first time I learned Dad was not always in control of things.

From Gloria's farm, I flew to Maine to stay with a friend. I sat on rocks above the chilly blue Atlantic and watched brown sea ducks ride the surf and worried about the smallest one, who rode low in the water, tilted forward as if he were not properly inflated.

Here I am again, out on the edge of the herd, observing and analyzing, I thought. As a kid, my human family often felt like a careening and crashing runaway, a parent at the reins but not in control.

What has made us horsegirls? The stability, peace and companionship that horses offer us in such a situation? Why are we not frightened away when accidents happen? Gloria, perhaps one of the biggest risk-takers in terms of equipment and potential disaster in her sport, did not suffer a runaway in her childhood. And I have, but stayed with it. That's what we do, all we can ever do. And it is, ultimately, what we want to do.

CHAPTER 12

Horsegirls Go to the Movies

"If you like horses, your life changes forever. You can't sleep or eat or be a very good cowgirl without your trusty pal by your side at all times."

~Bonnie Timmons, *Hold Your Horses*

Robert Redford's voltage is undimmed by the years. As he yanked his gloves from his chaps and pulled them on (in horse movies, the action starts when the gloves come on), Lucy and I gasped, rolled our eyes at each other and sank deeper in our seats. To our mutual relief, however, *The Horse Whisperer* doesn't stoop to sell itself with sex. It is about several kinds of love, most pivotally that of a girl for a horse.

We had planned to deal with the accident scene that happens in the early moments of the film by sending our husbands in first. They would sit through the tough stuff and fetch us from the lobby when it was over. But months went by, and that foursome date never came to pass. So one early autumn afternoon, Lucy and I went off to a two-dollar matinée, smuggling pita sandwiches and iced tea into the theater under our jackets.

"How are we gonna deal with the first part?" she asked me.

"We're late already, maybe it's over," I suggested.

There were other couples scattered in the theater, all pairs of women except for one elderly man.

We rustled into our seats just in time for the amputation announcement scene. I held my deli napkin over my eyes so I wouldn't see the screen, but I peeked anyway: bloody horse standing in a winter creek beneath a bridge; battered daughter in a hospital bed; pale-faced girl on crutches gawked at by schoolmates; one-legged girl weeping in bed as she watched videos of herself and her horse, a gelding named Pilgrim, riding a jump course.

"Which is harder for you, this or the horse scenes?" I whispered to Lucy as the screen filled with distressed parents at their daughter's bedside. Should they put the traumatized horse down as the trainer recommended?

"I have a daughter, so this is harder," said Lucy.

"I can't eat," she added, putting her sandwich back into the bag and stuffing it under her seat. "You'll have to put me down if anything happens to Lily."

"I will not!" I whispered back, my cheeks wet with tears.

"That's it," Lucy declared. "Lily's not riding. We're going to have to build a tennis court."

We sniffled until the scene when the mother, a hotshot Manhattan magazine editor, trailers the horse, the girl and their mammoth cases of post-traumatic stress disorder cross country. She does so hoping a legendary horseman (played with charming understatement by Redford—am I too, too obviously smitten?) will restore the horse and heal her despondent daughter.

"I want a man like that!" Lucy whispered to me as Redford counsels the mother, saying "Don't let her push you away."

I made it through my sandwich, blowing my nose into my pickle-scented napkin, but it took Lucy nearly an hour into the film before she could finish hers.

A few days prior to our movie date, Brad the Farrier—as Lucy and I call him—was bending over Lucy's gelding's hoof with a couple of horseshoe nails clenched between his lips, tapping on a shoe.

"That '*Horse Whisperer*' is a chick flick," he mumbled. He says this half to provoke me, as he trims Burt, whose undersized hooves are all too typical of modern Quarter Horses. I have known Brad so long that his red hair and mustache have gone to gray. He is notably short and makes self-deprecating jokes about his parents being elves, but he is so much in demand that he books appointments weeks ahead. And he won't work at some stables.

"Bad Zen," he pronounces.

Over the years, Brad and I have talked movies, books and horses to the t-tak, t-tak, t-tak of his shoeing hammer. This day's topic was *Zen and the Art of Motorcycle Maintenance* by local author Robert Pirsig while Brad pared off hoof and sluiced iodine on a thrushy frog.

"My wife and daughter tricked me," he said. "They said they had a Clint Eastwood flick to watch, and I sat down, and it was that 'Bridges of Wisconsin' or something. I said, 'Where's the shooting?'"

"So murder, car chases, and things getting blown up are fine, but not emotion?" I poked at him.

"About getting your heart broke, anything but that," he said.

And here on the screen is Redford, powerfully dignified, quietly dashing, masterfully working rope and horse in a round pen, squatting silently in a pasture, communicating confidence to the battered and distrustful Pilgrim. And, in the end, getting his heart broke.

I would have dumped that Manhattan editor job in a New York minute.

Yet I acknowledged, between blowing my nose, that here was one more movie to join the pantheon that extols man's relationship to horses—but less so woman's.

Other than *National Velvet*, have there been hit mainstream films that show a girl or woman riding, teaching, displaying mastery? In *The Black Stallion*, it's Alec and his old trainer. In *Phar Lap, Seabiscuit* and *Secretariat,* it's more trainers, grooms, jockeys and owners, all male (except Penny Chenery, owner of Secretariat) *The Man From Snowy River, Hidalgo* and *War Horse* deserve the accolades and ongoing popularity. I watched *Buck* (the story of horse trainer Buck Brannaman) twice and probably would see it again.

But where are we?

Girls are so often fed *My Little Pony* cartoons and rainbow unicorn slush. It's a wonder that millions of us make our way to real horses at all.

Yet in the audiences of horse films, reaching for their tissues, it's far and away girls and women.

The term "horse whisperer" was codified in the 1995 book by Nicholas Evans, which became the tenth best-selling novel in the U.S. that year. The 1998 film of the same name followed, distilling the essence of training techniques used by the handful of (almost exclusively) men teaching "natural horsemanship": Buck Brannaman, Monty Roberts, Pat Parelli, John Lyons, et al. What they do is use quiet, subtle body language rather than force to communicate with a horse.

The demographics of their followers included the late Queen Elizabeth II, perhaps the ultimate horsegirl, who invited Monty Roberts to her stables and to her ninetieth birthday celebration.

The whispering isn't just one way. Horses whisper to us as well in the eloquence of an eye, the prick of an ear, the shiver of a shoulder.

So who is in the audience for the horse whispering clinics, for the demonstrations, and for any and all horse movies? Horsewomen, horsegirls, a few men and a special, somewhat annoying subset of horse nerds.

You do not want to sit next to me during films in which there are horses unless you are as batty as I am, because I am a horse nerd and I mutter. We may be enjoying any of a half-dozen nice Jane Austen films or something from the dear and delicious *Downton Abbey*, and I am scrutinizing the equines first and actors second.

"Historically incorrect bit!" I say, pouncing.

"Same pair of Shires in every scene," I note, aloud.

"Hey, he can actually ride," I say, approving actor Cillian Murphy bareback on a tall, big-boned gray in *Peaky Blinders*.

"Oooh, Andalusians or Lusitanos?" I exclaim, certain that the capering horses in a *Musketeers* film are Iberian. Or "Great—they are using actual Highland horses!" approvingly as the hunt scene in the Scottish Highlands in *Downton Abbey* unfolds.

Anachronism may not bother most normal humans, but I am a horsegirl and a horse nerd. Jamie Fraser's charm notwithstanding, I notice four-legged actors more than the two-legged ones,.

"Dammit, that's not a Colonial-era horse!" I hiss during the *Outlander* episodes when some of the Scots are aboard what appears to be tall baroque breeds.

Then there are the period horse-drawn vehicles. Okay, what is that? I think, trying to recall what distinguishes each vehicle and name them as they wheel into the scene: barouche, vis-à-vis, hansom cab, Victoria, roof seat break.

"Friesians again," I say, with a sigh. Not that I don't like them, but what I call "The Ladyhawke Effect" has meant that for the last decade or three, a disproportionately high number of horses in film, particularly films set in Europe, are Friesians. It began almost certainly with the 1985 romantic fantasy film *Ladyhawke* starring Michelle Pfeiffer and Rutger Hauer. In actuality, the high-headed black Dutch carriage horses were not present in every pirate port, castle, country market town or battle. When it comes to most films, however, with horses as with women, a certain kind of beauty often lands the roles.

To us, the young, the middle-aged, and the elder horsegirls in the theater, or watching on Netflix, they are all beautiful.

There is some progress from this. Lately, everyone gushes over the CBC series *Heartland*, which features a female trainer and is Friesian-free, as it is set on a Western ranch.

So feed us more movies with horses, more TV series with good riders—we'll be there in the dark with our sodas and popcorn, sniffling, cheering and eating it all up.

CHAPTER 13

Horse Worship

"One of the earliest religious disappointments in a young girl's life devolves upon her unanswered prayer for a horse."

~ Phyllis Theroux

We roll out in the morning chill from Louisville toward Lexington on ribbon-narrow roads past porticoed houses, through pastures rich in oaks, buckeyes, and drooping walnut trees and, of course, horses. I am on a bus with several dozen women sweeping through the gentle hills of Kentucky, taking part in what is arguably the pilgrimage of devotees to all things Horse.

This is the vaunted bluegrass region where the limestone underpinnings are supposed to give sturdier bone to the "blood horses" (Thoroughbreds) born and raised there.

Our guide, a lean, middle-aged man in a neat navy-blue blazer, knows his stuff; he leavens this stable tour with information on tobacco and bourbon as well as horse breeder gossip and history. The bus swoops and dives through green and twisting roadways, and we all listen carefully to his talk, punctuating with our collective murmur as we pass another herd of brood mares and foals: "Ohh cuuute!"

Past Three Chimneys Farm, Woodstock Farm and Alchemy Farm, past bays, sorrels and blacks, our constant refrain is a soft, collective "Oooooh! Awwwww! Mmmm!" and once a collective "Yeeha!" as we watch a gray and a cream horse sprint together across the bright morning grass.

We are teens to middle-aged to seniors, most of us wear our hair a little longer than optimum for our years and every woman has something pretty about her eyes. And to a woman, when we see foals scoot like fawns over the wet fields it's "Oh, teeny ones" and a general sigh of desire and yearning.

The tour is an option during the four-day all-horses-all-day indulgence held in Louisville, an exposition known as Equitana USA. Equitana was born in 1972 in Essen, Germany, and then launched in 1996 in Louisville, Kentucky, with 600 vendors from 18 countries. The biennial event swells annually and now covers several hundred acres. Tens of thousands of people, most of them women and girls, watch horses perform, feast on displays, sign up for riding trips and buy equine paraphernalia.

It is billed as an all-breeds trade exhibition show; however, my teenage goddaughter, Allie, and I are two of the congregants, and we are clearly in a state of adoration.

Down the exhibition hall aisles I race with Allie, snickering at T-shirts that declare, "So Many Horses, So Little Time," "Barn Goddess," and "My Husband Says if I Go to One More Horse Show He's Gonna Leave Me. I'm Sure Gonna Miss Him."

Around us, women and girls are wriggling into chaps, scooping up riding breeches with tiny rubber horses galloping over the thigh and seat, draping their necks with silver Pegasus earrings and necklaces, swinging their legs over new saddles, and carrying off bags of riding videos, bridles, and saddle blankets.

I try riding the mechanical roping horse, flailing the rope foolishly and to no avail as the mechanical calf bolts forward, and Allie gets pink with laughter.

This may look like shopping, but it is worship. Silly at times—leather toilet seat covers embossed with horse images? Umbrellas decorated with velveteen horse ears? But worship it is.

In the seventeen thousand years since the horse images in the caves of Lascaux and Trois-Frères, France, were painted, and eight centuries after Pope Calixtus II decreed, "No more ceremonies in the cave with the horse pictures," women have their Notre Dame, their Mecca, their Jerusalem in horse expos, and their little chapels in horse barns and backyard stables everywhere.

Our horse paintings, jewelry, T-shirts and tattoos do more than evoke something we love to ride. They seem to be icons of an animal that is also a noble being, or perhaps a nobler self, that we venerate.

That evening after the tour, Allie and I took our seats in the rafters of a sold-out show called "The Mane Event," a Las-Vegas-style revue. We were next to a 68-year-old woman from Indiana. We talked (horses, naturally) for fifteen minutes while awaiting the opening act.

"You can stay with me if you're in town. I have a big house," she offered. I felt suddenly like my dad, whose Masonic ring earned him rides, rooms and meals when he was a young naval enlistee hitchhiking during World War II. I, too, am in an ancient quasi-religious order, a sorority mostly, where the stable/chapel doors are open to those who know the secret code.

That women worship horses annually at Equitana, at the Equine Affaire and dozens of other horse expos around the world should be no surprise.

In our shared strength and sweetness, vigor and vulnerability, there is some equation of childhood, of love, nature and estrogen that draws women to horses. And then there is the shopping!

American women are buying themselves horses in unprecedented numbers, many of us at the biological crossroads of mid-life. That is when a great portion of us begin to take medically prescribed hormones supplied largely by pregnant mare urine on so-called PMU farms.

"Tell 'em it's horse piss," said the woman in the seat in front of us at the Equitana show. "They may not believe you or care that the mares are in tie stalls with tubes hooked to them or that most of the foals are killed every fall. But they probably won't like knowing they're eating pills made from horse piss."

Perhaps it's not surprising that one elixir of femininity should come from mares, as if horses, distilled, should be in our blood. Certainly the passion is there in each generation of girls, who point out car windows at age three and coo "Horsie, horsie!" or "Neigh neigh!" much as Allie and I did on the tour bus rolling through bluegrass country earlier that day.

Who do we think we are? For a while, for many of us, it's a horse.

It is play and more than play: we clatter plastic model horses across tabletops around imaginary paddocks and into imaginary stables. We canter and paw, snort and prance in a dance in which we evoke the horse ourselves, grass-stained knees transmuted into the hooves of fiery steeds, our ponytails into luxurious horse manes. We set up jumps made of sofa cushions or branches and jump them down the hallway or across the backyard.

The standard little boy fascination with dinosaurs doesn't compare. Boys usually don't think they are dinosaurs or keep dinosaurs when they grow up.

Who indeed are we, the obsessed, the possessed?

Perhaps we have never needed them more, not as commercial transport or military might (the last cavalry charge, by doomed Polish nobility, took place in 1939 in Krojanty, Pomerania). What sort of spiritual nourishment are they providing now? And where are the congregations meeting?

Now that America is no longer predominately agricultural, the great majority of horses are kept in boarding stables. Boarding stables I've visited by the hundreds confirm that women are the majority of clients, so much so that there's often not a single male boarder. I always ask, because I can't always see every boarder.

What I do see are sites of veneration replete with their own language, which is obscure to outsiders. We identify ourselves by our stables much as Catholics used to describe where they live by parish.

"Betsy and Amanda are over at Ernie and Marilyn's, and of course, Michelle is still there," or "Kathy was at Max's for a while" and "Jan moved, but Allie and Genevieve and Olivia stayed at Kelly's" meaning those women keep their horses (and often the heart of their social lives) at stables owned by Ernie and Marilyn, Max or Kelly.

Hanging out in the barn with other devotees is not exactly like being at the alley with your bowling team. It's more like a congregation replete with a tack room or lounge with sacramental wine and margaritas, pans of brownies, crockpots of meatballs or stew. It's a weekly ritual that supplies joy and refreshment in nature and in slowing to horse tempo.

"The horse, with its slower pace, symbolizes reversion to the rhythm and harmony of the natural order," according to the late Dr. Elizabeth Lawrence, cultural anthropologist and horse–human relations specialist at Tufts University. Lawrence believes horses are a way of marking transition, that it is no accident that so many riders are girls eleven to fourteen or so, on the cusp of womanhood.

Horses carry women to new dimensions and old, and women return the favor. It is far and away females who study and teach horse-related tai chi, enroll in yoga for equestrians, practice equine-facilitated therapy for troubled youngsters and adults and run volunteer programs in riding for the disabled. Women train in whole new specialty medical practices of horse chiropractic, equine acupuncture and massage therapy.

We adorn ourselves with the creatures we adore, and we also adorn the creatures: Women and girls have propelled a boom in horse cosmetics ranging from mane and tail hair conditioners, pots of glitter to be painted onto hooves or combed into manes and tails, decorative stencils shaved or brushed onto the hair of a rump or shoulder. Our need to decorate and beautify is also revamping and increasing tack sales resulting in lighter, less expensive saddles—also much more expensive saddles for those who can demand them.

The tack stores of my childhood chiefly offered leather goods in brown, russet and black, riding pants in buff, black and indigo, conservative colors in saddle pads. Today, all colors of the rainbow show up in jeans, breeches, jackets, horse blankets, even vet wrap for injured legs.

That shift is seen everywhere, not just retail: It's mostly women who write, film, and blog about them as well. At American Horse Publications (AHP), a Charlottesville, Virginia-based organization of 350 media professionals and publications, executive director Chris Brune tells me that there were more men than women writing for equine media when she became involved in the '70s.

"That changed quickly," she said. "Our membership is predominantly women. The AHP Facebook page audience is 80% women, 20% men; the analytics on the AHP website audience is 62% women, 28% men."

And so it is that horses, humbly used for millennia for transport, competition, and (shudder) food are now in their glory, in very large part thanks to the female affinity for them.

Horses lead to non-verbal pure joy, provide an antidote to malls, computers, cars and freeways. Horses are the cure for the anomie of "what remains when we're so human we only live in mind and talk," as poet Lisa Lewis writes in "The Lamed Mare."

For the women on that Kentucky stable tour, joyfully chorusing over every horse, pony or donkey we pass, equines are something to nurture that nurtures us in return.

When Allie and I return to Minnesota, I seek out Jungian psychologist Lyn Cowan for her take on the whole phenomenon.

Horses give us back our bodies, freedom and power, and something more, something transcendent, explains Cowan. She is not the only psychologist to tell me this.

"In riding you become nothing but body," Cowan said. "It's only physical, but at the same time for me it is such a mystical rapture that I am actually only spirit. The simultaneity of that, I know no other way to do it."

Perhaps the Paleolithic artists painted cave walls out of the same impulse felt by every girl who doodles horses in the margins of her notebook, or sneaks a look at the DreamHorse.com site on her laptop. We are all perhaps dreaming of a non-critical love, a love with a kind and tender heart, a love that can, quite literally, carry us away.

The cave artists might have been conjuring food as well as expressing worship, but it's not much of a stretch to imagine that friends crowded around as someone drew on the rock face by torchlight, and that they had the same response as the horsewomen on our bus in Kentucky—"Ohhh cuuuute!

CHAPTER 14

Genes, Gender, and Other Beings

"What can I give you to explain this horsey phenomenon? Casual observation? If so, let me tell you that it's real: More than half of all little girls in the industrialized world one sudden day fall madly, truly, deeply in love with horses."

~ **Melissa Holbrook Pierson,**
Dark Horses and Black Beauties: Animals, Women, a Passion

When I finally caught up with Maxine Kumin, she was recovering from a near-fatal carriage driving accident in which she broke, among other things, her neck.

Kumin was a poetry professor and winner of the 1973 Pulitzer Prize for Poetry. For many years, she raised Arabians on her small farm in New Hampshire, where she was poet laureate of the state from 1989 to 1994. She was also consultant in poetry to the Library of Congress, an honor later known as poet laureate of the United States.

I sought her out because she is a born horsewoman and has written about her horses in ways I tremble to read, so spare and evocative they are.

"My husband shares my madness," she said. "We were both competitive trail riders for ten years and logged hundreds of miles, and we turned to driving after our arthritis became painful. Then we did competitive distance driving, where the horse who almost killed me won everything in sight. Then we went to event driving. My kids were after me to give it up, but I told them that when I'm killed at least Mother will have died doing something she loved. Such hubris!"

In her essay "Silver Snaffles," first published in 1973 in *Ms.* magazine as "Why is it That Girls Love Horses?" she talked about interspecies communication and bonding that is the basis of human love of horses.

Kumin titled the piece after a novel by British writer Primrose Cumming about a happy world of young girls and their ponies. It was a fantasy into which Kumin regularly escaped as a child, just as my friends and I had done, just as I see girls and women doing now.

The powerful force between girls and horses is a huge mystery to which she has no answer, she confessed, although she has been celebrating, probing, and describing that mystery in prose and poetry since she was a child. Its force struck her early, as it usually does.

"When I was very young, I wrote 'The Confidante,' a poem in which I describe being lifted on my father's livery horse," she recalled. "I was probably four or five. It was the sensation of my hands on this damp neck, and I fell in love with the whole idea."

She made scrapbooks of pictures of horses, just as I did. And she likens her attraction to worship. I have to agree. It is a worship that does not preclude other theologies, one perhaps more raw and, for many of us, more accessible.

Why is there currently such a strong and rising interest in horses? And why is ownership of horses increasing, especially among women, I asked her.

"Partly it's the economy," said Kumin, "that makes it possible for all these dressage queens to purchase enormous horses they are scared to ride anywhere except the confines of a dressage ring."

And for the far greater number of us to have a horse on a more modest level, too, I thought.

Partly, it's birth control, which gives us the ability to regulate our time and finances. And of course, it's those finances; women are a larger part of the workforce than ever. While I won't be able to prove females have always had a passion for horses, I suspect the social situation has never been more favorable to making our dreams reality. We marry later, divorce more often, or stay single—there is no one to deter us from being horsegirls.

Kumin sees nothing special in single women having horses. And she agrees we are drawn to animals in general and horses most keenly by far.

"Horsewomen are animal people, they don't have just horses," she said.

"An awful lot of unmarried women have cats and dogs—any animal."

This was to come out in the open with a comic twist in the presidential race of 2024, when "childless cat ladies" became an internet meme. And this is true of nearly every horsewoman or girl I meet, some of whom have whole packs of dogs (usually rescued) or barnfuls of cats (ditto).

Women often make the best trainers for problem horses, Kumin told me, citing women's "empathy, subtlety, ability to read the nuance of difference that leads to change; women's gift of timing; women's instinct for nurturing as qualities that make them widely successful" on breeding farms, in show rings, in the racing world, and as riding instructors. Somehow the notion of improving performance by developing a trusting partnership between horse and human elicits a readier response from women than from some men.

When we spoke, Kumin still owned four horses, but since her accident, she will probably never drive or ride again, she admitted gloomily. Her devotion to horses even now that she is injured, however, confirms they are some kind of essential balm, even if one can't ride or drive them.

"Today, horses still enter into a lot of what I think and feel and do," she said. "I still somehow manage to get to the barn in the morning and feed them. I use a ski pole to be sure I don't slip and break my neck again. I'm not ready to turn my back on them. They are family members. I wouldn't sell my child, therefore why would I sell my horse?"

The grip that horses have on me, on this poet-farmer, and on millions of other females is, well, ineffable, she has concluded.

"I'm not any closer to understanding it now than then," she said.

I eagerly searched out her poem "Women and Horses" hoping to find she expressed it there, only to find it is about the aftermath of World War II, in which many of her relatives were killed. And yet the poem concludes, "*Let us see life again, nevertheless, in the words of Isaac Babel as a meadow over which women and horses wander.*"

Despite humans' interminable insistence on war, that meadow, perhaps, was the best life she could imagine, too.

Never content with only part of the puzzle, after Kumin I turned to another scholar, Tufts University cultural anthropologist Dr. Elizabeth Lawrence. Lawrence, a veterinarian who lives on a small farm in Connecticut, was happy to help me noodle the topic.

"I wonder and wonder and wonder—it's such a puzzlement," she told me. As one of the foremost scholars of horses and human behavior, she has studied horses and rodeos, horses and Romany people, and the role of horses in the Crow Native American tribe.

Her equivalent to my Gabe was Bonnie, a delicate and beautiful Morgan mare she purchased when the horse was five. She owned Bonnie until the mare died at 31, a long life typical of that breed. She has been horseless since then. Some part of me not far from the surface has never recovered from losing Gabe, although I have gone on to have more horses. So I was curious that she could live without them. How is it possible, having loved and been loved this way, to be without a horse?

"I would get an old horse maybe, but I like to have an animal forever, so to undertake a young one now would be wrong," she explained. "It's harder to get over a horse's death than almost anything. I'm not saying they are more important than people, but the death of a horse is something really terrible, something on a different order than human companions."

It was Lawrence who imparted one of the things I dreaded to hear confirmed: "I don't think you ever get over it," she confided.

"I remember the first time I saw a horse from the backseat of my father's old car," she said. "I was very little, but I fell in love, madly in love. I had such a bad case of horse-itis and never stopped having it."

We have both noticed there seem to be two general types of horse-loving females. As she put it, "There are women who have horse-itis and suddenly get a boyfriend and don't have it. There are others who, if they get a boyfriend, he has to like horses or else."

Lawrence has witnessed how some experts oversimplify the phenomenon or are dismissive, even insulting.

"When I wrote the rodeo book, a woman veterinarian and animal behaviorist told me 'Well, it's just if you're brought up on a ranch, that's what you do.' They want to make it simple, and it isn't."

"I once went to a conference, an overview of human–horse relationships where a well-known male veterinarian and author was quite rude and pooh-poohed it all," she continued. "He said that for young girls, 'Horses are a wonderful training for marriage.' In his opinion, it was all maternal instinct—misdirected by implication—and once girls 'got sense,' they would turn it to children. He completely looked down on it."

Lawrence doesn't presume to have fully penetrated the horses–girls–women phenomenon, but she speculates that some of it may be cultural, some genetic, some aesthetic ("and women have more aesthetic sense").

She suspects some of the enthusiasm for riding may be girls' traditional exclusion from many other sports. Is it our default sport? I disagreed, silently: Every bit of evidence I have shows me that while many of us choose to compete in equestrian events it is far more than a sport.

At the time I met her, Title IX (the 1972 U.S. federal law that prohibits sex-based discrimination at schools that receive federal funds) was not widely enforced. Many schools are not in full compliance even now, a half-century later. American girls enjoy widening access and support for taking part in any and all sports except perhaps American football. Yet that has not noticeably diminished their innate ardor for all things equine, we agreed.

"I'm a cultural anthropologist, but I don't believe everything is culture; certain things are built into humans," Lawrence affirmed. "In our culture, the love of horses seems to be something that many women have and men don't. As for other horsey cultures, the British have always liked horses a lot, yet with a kind of domination, not equality."

Lawrence seemed both intellectually keen and precise and extremely gentle, and she confirmed it both through our conversations and in what she revealed about her own style of riding. With her beloved Bonnie, she said, she never rode her as a ruler, never insisted on being in charge.

"I broke the first rule of riding: Be the boss, never let her get away with anything," she admitted. "When we rode, I let my mare pick which way to go."

As for the effect of horses on the dynamic within a human couple, she speculated that it might be useful to compare it to a marriage where someone likes, say, boats, and the spouse is indifferent to them.

"There are many men crazy about boats. They are gone all weekend, and if the woman doesn't like it, it's very threatening. Horses are much easier. Mine was in my backyard, so I'm not gone, but it would be different if I were on the show circuit.

"If we can crystallize the thing going on here, we must be getting into the very nature of femininity," Lawrence said. "Something in females, something about the essence of femininity is answering and interacting strongly with a horse."

Perhaps it's related to "girls' general greater communicativeness," she added.

"In her book, *In a Different Voice*, Carol Gilligan comes to the conclusion that girls are different from boys, that girls are more communicative and that it's not just a conditioned thing," said Lawrence. "I wonder if they confide in a horse more than boys do. In our culture, most boys hide their pain. I've heard a lot of young girls whose parents divorce say they feel bad and they can talk to a horse. Do boys do that as much? I don't have proof, but Gilligan says girls care more about interaction with other beings."

Before we have a real horse, she noted, we interact with toy equine beings.

Like many girls, Lawrence and I collected model horses from the Woolworth's and Benjamin Franklin stores. Some of our dime store horses are now in antique shops, and I spot others in junk stores. Still others became cult collectibles: I'm thinking of Breyer model horses here, which even have their own convention of collectors and fans: 30,000 showed up at the 2022 BreyerFest in the Kentucky Horse Park in Lexington, Kentucky

Kumin continued, "A scientist would ask, 'Why don't girls and women turn to a dog or a cat?' I have very aesthetic leanings, and the beauty of the horse is a tremendous factor for me—the flowing manes, their faces. And not all dogs are beautiful."

"It isn't that we're all a great sisterhood of like souls," she cautioned. "I know some nasty horsewomen, too, people who are very much in it for the control. I never felt I was. I can't relate to people who are very bossy and even cruel to horses. Many horse people are pretty harsh; they trade in a horse if they are showing and think another one is better."

Lawrence used the example of Tennessee Walkers, a gaited breed whose natural high action is often enhanced for something called "big lick" competitions by painful mechanical means: nails, caustic substances, and even golf balls in their hooves. We had both seen the undercover tapes that reveal this and heard the justifications that competitors use, including "it's a Southern tradition."

"Those horses are tortured to a terrific degree, and not just by men but by the women who show them, too," Lawrence said. "Clearly they don't relate to horses in the way we're discussing. They might say 'I love horses,' but I think they are getting power or control."

She made other distinctions among horsewomen: For some of us, any horse will do. We simply want to be around horses or work with them, but we don't love an individual equine. For others, the deep relationship with one horse is what matters, a kindhearted equality of relationship, something in a different dimension than categorial horsecraziness.

"My focus was always on one," she said, referring to her mare, Bonnie. "Horses are very vulnerable, so sensitive and so willing. And I am so sensitive about them. I can't even read *Black Beauty*, because it just kills me."

In the way that equines take a range of forms from wild to tame, Lawrence told me, they represent and display all stages in the transition between nature and culture.

Her research in rodeo culture shows that men associate both women and broncs with unpredictability. Women and wild horses are viewed as closer to nature than to culture, which is considered tame and predictable. In professional rodeo culture, bronc riding is still almost exclusively reserved for men, with the underlying assumption that the "wild" must be conquered. This is a totally masculine pursuit, Lawrence found.

I am more literal: horses are simply beautiful, and they call to me in a primal and gratifying way.

I take her point that horses represent nature in their utterly unpretentious, sensual being—the sound of their hooves, the rhythm of their movements, their snorts and shivers and sighs, and, yes, the bucking and farting. We don't often think about it, but to some women they may represent the sea or evoke the heartbeat, among other things.

During the years I was a carriage driver in downtown St. Paul, I got through many cold December and January evenings by singing to myself. Frequently, it was Beach Boys stuff. If my customers were not the carol-singing type, I sang or hummed or listened to hoofbeats or to the rhythm of sleigh bells worn in a thick strap around the barrels of my black Percherons.

I drove five or six different draft horses for the carriage company, and in those hours of listening I noted that no two walks or trots were the same. A stately mare named Karen walked with a direct, unornamented one-two, one-two. A chunky little gelding named Bob had a different tempo, something soft and shuffly, *popf-popf-popf-popf.*

Sometimes my partner for the night was Jill, a high-headed, prancy black Percheron–Shire cross, the big mama of the herd. Watching her powerful hips, I noticed Jill's walk was easiest to track when the bells on her ribs swayed to her steps: ah-ONE-ay-and-ah TWO-ay-and-ah. Jill's syncopation reminded me of the women in Rio de Janeiro with their fluid, unabashed shimmy and bounce.

I am not alone in responding to horse rhythms.

One winter evening, a newspaper colleague came for her first carriage ride. Sally had ridden with me for years, and now she and her husband Jim piled excitedly into the upholstered seats of the vis-à-vis behind me, and we set off, sleigh bells jingling. When they emerged half an hour later, Sally looked up at me on the box and said, "It is so relaxing! The hoofbeats are the exact tempo of your heart."

Rhythm is what we get before we have a vocabulary, something transcendent, and it speaks to us in the bodies of animals as well as in our bodies.

The February she was five, I took my niece Zosha out to the stable for her first ride on Smokey. She was squirmy and chatty with delight, her grins punctuated by gaps where she'd recently lost baby teeth. Up and down the driveway in the slush, I led Smokey, Zosha high on his back in a yellow parka and green plush cap, her arms spread like wings.

"One more ride, Zosh," said her mother, my sister Gayle, who has allergies and sneezes heartily just being in view of a horse.

"Two! Two more rides, and then I get to brush him," she negotiated. As we descended the driveway for about the fourth time, she confided "I like the rhythm of his hooves."

Is it the beat? It is for some of us something stamped into our collective unconsciousness millennia ago: Ah one, ah two, lub-dub, lub-dub. Mother, the heart heard from within the womb, the very first tympani of life, heartbeat, hoofbeat, horsebeat.

In spring, I drove carriages for high school proms, round and round a few downtown blocks, hauling teenage foursomes in formal dress. By 10 p.m., most of the girls were limping or walking barefoot and carrying their new shoes. One evening, I spotted three kids: a massive girl in black taffeta who looked less like a high school junior than an opera diva; a slender girl whose champagne-colored silk evening shift cascaded close to her body, and a stout boy in a tuxedo escorting them both.

As the horse and I approached, all three began to dance, bending at the waist, leaning, stepping barefoot, wearing expressions of delight and surprise.

"We're dancing to the horse's feet!" shouted the biggest girl.

And what could be more natural?

One evening, driving Bob on my usual route behind the elegant old Saint Paul Hotel, I spotted a young man in outsize shirt and jeans waiting at a bus stop. The first time we circled the block, he silently took up our tempo, striding next to us on the sidewalk, matching Bob's pace and neck movement. On our next pass, he let loose with an impromptu rap song in horse-walking tempo celebrating the horse, the horse's neck, head, feet. To Bob's rubber-shod clopping beat, he danced along the sidewalk beside us.

So what is it? Mothers, fathers, genes, rhythm, pure love, power, control, and/or a sense of safety (or defiance of it) all seem to go into the amalgam.

To get at the immensity of the feeling and weight, the deep-rooted awe women in particular have for horses, I decided to look at not just the place horses occupy in our biology, language, and culture but also in our psyches.

Getting away from word-linked meaning and closer to sound is a special interest of Mary Lynn Kittelson, a Minnesota Jungian analyst and psychologist. Kittelson and I met over coffee. She is tall and soft spoken, with straight gray hair and striking hazel eyes. I talked horses and showed photos of mine while she listened carefully.

"We believe it is we humans who control and affect animals, and perhaps in the fleshly sense, we do," she told me, once we had eased away from our introductions. "We breed, train, sell, euthanize, even eat them, but animals shape our consciousness as well."

She is interested in animals as "helping us into more soul," said Kittelson, author of *Sounding the Soul: The Art of Listening.*

"Animals are incredibly overlooked as forming us," she said. "We reduce them to instinct or drive, but what interests me is the imaginative experience of them. Not that they aren't out there and need our concern, and we can relate with them in a real way. Something about caring for them, the inner energies that go with the outer relationship, helps us relate to ourselves and everything else."

She cited sound as one of the ways animals affect humans: the sounds horses make, the vibratory experience, the chest cavity resonance of their voices and feet, the soft nicker, snort and whinny, the neigh and scream.

When I questioned her about the relationships between girls and horses, she went straight to the unicorn, my private totem beginning in junior high school.

"The unicorn is really a very fierce animal and will only become un-dangerous if it lays its head in the lap of a virgin," Kittelson explained. "In some myths, the virgin has to kill the unicorn. I wonder if that's not a male coming in. Women are more tamers, men more in hunting mode. The main theme of the virgin is, in a sense, a psychic virgin, which is a woman who knows herself."

The "virginity" of a young woman with the unicorn, she said, isn't sexual, but about relatedness to her true self, her real soul self.

That posed another question: are horsegirls and women, as I have seen, more sturdily self-confident, less willing to capitulate to the wishes or plans of partners or those who want something else? Do we know better, or earlier, who we are because of our attachment to equines? Do horses clarify our definition of ourselves?

"That's in a way what adolescence is about, not to mention the rest of life," said Kittelson. "It's somehow ringing true to your virginity, to who you are in your core."

I brought the topic to Lynn Baskfield, a coach who lives near Santa Fe, New Mexico, and has conducted equine-facilitated workshops in Brazil and Australia as well as around the U.S.

Many of her events are open to men, although, Lynn tells me, those who attend are there because their corporation booked all of its employees.

"Horses are a feminine archetype," Lynn explains. "They are borderline animals that take us to the dreamtime, like dolphins with their qualities of freedom, beauty, power and courage. Men are more mechanistic, and it is harder for some of them to open their hearts to hear messages. We hear the call, and most men do get it eventually—the idea of listening to these things."

"It's a little esoteric, but women are body creatures, and the goddess cultures talk about the body as place of creativity where the divine dwells," Lynn added. "Horses bring us back to our bodies, and they are a way for young women to be called to that experience as expressive beings interconnected with a completely embodied being."

I am certainly in my body when I ride, although those who don't ride, who are not born horsegirls, think it's more like being out of our minds.

Alright, I am listening.

CHAPTER 15

The Curse of A Tender Heart

"I spent money that I did not have, giving up many things, but all these things are not worth even one special moment with my horse. He is not a means of transport or a piece of iron with wheels, it is the lost part of my soul and my spirit."

~ Cindy Keisling,
"The Dream That Many Will Not Understand"

"This is unsustainable," said Kris, my financial advisor, sitting across the conference table from me.

Over decades of our quarterly meetings, she had never before used the term.

But then, I had never before confessed.

Online late at night, weeping with rage, I click away, sending funds to horse rescue groups who try to get them out of slaughter buyer pens: $30 here, $100 there, $10 when I pull myself back. Sharing madly, tagging and annoying friends who often unfriend me, pestering and pleading with the world to do something—do something, goddammit!—for the horses.

Along with the little gifts from uncountable thousands of us doing likewise, the donations trickle out to save Standardbreds, driving horses who give their all on the race track and then serve Amish families for years. It trickles to summer camp horses and ponies who introduce children to riding and carry them safely nose to tail on the trail or around a ring.

It trickles to racing Thoroughbreds that are deemed too slow or are injured and are shunted off the backside. It trickles to pregnant mares and unwanted donkeys and Mustangs of all ages and sexes rounded up on our public lands and dumped by the Bureau of Land Management (BLM). It trickles to "recipient mares" inseminated with the fertilized eggs of champion show mares so owners can create as many pricey foals as possible and then toss the real mamas away when they are no longer able to carry foals. Many are backyard horses whose owners couldn't be bothered to build fences or get a colt gelded so their mares are all pregnant.

All of these are sent to auctions where often the meat men get them cheap, hold them until they gather enough—about 35—to fill up a tractor trailer, then haul them to slaughter plants in Mexico or Canada.

This happens without the knowledge of most Americans; among those who do know, according to a 2022 national survey by the Humane Society of the United States (HSUS), 83% support banning horse slaughter for human consumption.

One year, in a particular fury compounded by irrational confidence in the stock market, I donated more than I earned, dipping into funds stashed away for retirement.

That year at our quarterly meeting, Kris retained her neutral voice and expression and said, "Do you think you can control this?"

Maybe. Then again, maybe not.

I look at equines online the way some males look at pornography. Not with that furtive, erotic charge, but consistently and embarrassingly often. While the digital age has enabled many folks to play video games or solitaire compulsively, I peer into sites such as Border Horse Slaughter Rescue and SE Horses at Risk or Arabian Feedlot and Auction Horse Team Rescue. Mostly—well, daily—I visit any of a dozen rescue sites, the very last chance for a thrown-away donkey, pony, horse, miniature horse or mule.

For years, as a consequence, I have been giving money I didn't have to people I don't know for the benefit of horses I would never meet: Marion in Oregon, Robin in Alabama, Terra in Michigan, Pamela in California, Mary in Connecticut, Penny in Canada, Randi in Texas as well as to random and assorted others.

They all happen to be women. It's the "happen" that intrigues me.

In Pennsylvania, Leah, a rider who keenly monitors kill buyer pens and sales in the Northeast, has told me, "Yes, it's pretty much all women. It's so weird, I don't understand it." Leah doesn't just donate: she and her husband Chris scooped up a stunning bay Thoroughbred from a kill buyer pen and have showed him in the ribbons.

Out there beyond my computer screen, women (and a few men) form a staunch network who visit auctions and kill buyer pens, then post photos of the horses and their details online, begging for homes, for transport, for donations in attempts to get them out of the slaughter pipeline.

Sometimes I look at the postings and photos and weep, tears falling into the mixture of cat hair, toast crumbs and chocolate on my keyboard, and I suspect many others are doing likewise.

Mules, donkeys and miniature horses are in peril as well as horses and ponies. Some rescuers specialize in a region or a breed—draft horses or Thoroughbreds, for example. A few are registered 501-C3s, more are big-hearted types who can't stand by while equines are trucked to slaughter and butchered for sashimi and steaks in Japan, Korea and other markets.

There is no more glue factory or dog food factory involved: this is humans eating equines. It is miniature horses being sold to zoos for food for big cats. It is slender and speedy Arabians being chased by men on horseback who rope their front legs so they trip (often breaking legs or their necks) in an event called "horse tripping" in Mexican rodeos. It is 4.8 million donkeys being skinned (sometimes alive) annually for a Chinese folk medicine called *ejiao* made from the gelatin in their hides.

And then women got involved: Now, uncountable individual women or groups usually led by women are pushing back. Colby's Crew, a rescue based in Charlottesville, Virginia, has 408,000 followers on Facebook, 165,000 on Instagram and 2,900,000 on TikTok. It is named for a Dutch Harness gelding that founder Ally Smith saw online ready to load in the death truck at a Pennsylvania slaughter buyer facility. Ally got the big chestnut with the wide blaze to safety. He had been so traumatized that he was as dangerous as a feral stallion—striking, rearing, bolting. Ally spent months of gentle time with him, and Colby remains her heart horse and inspiration.

In addition to a diverse team of volunteers, Colby's Crew now has a staff of ten—"mostly women," she tells me—who help handle and adopt out their renovated rescues, which have reached an average of one or two a day. The effect of their energetic anti-slaughter campaign (the motto is "Not One More!") is clear: equine exports to slaughter in Canada were down 34 percent in 2023.

According to Ally, the single licensed slaughter holding facility on the East Coast (Pennsylvania) has reduced exports from its location by 89%.

And yet the slaughter continues: In 2023, 17,997 U.S. equines were shipped to their deaths in Mexico (to uninspected or unregulated plants) and another 2,373 were shipped to Canada, according to Fred Hudson, director of equine welfare for Animal Wellness Action.

What does rescue do for those of us who donate and adopt? Barbara McWhirter, a retired attorney in Connecticut, told me it fills a need to give.

"Horses allow me to act on a need to give to the point that every year I donate about $1,500 to rescue," said Barbara, who also adopted several horses. "It's a wicked need. I can't stop myself; the pain, the emotional overwhelmingness of the suffering of horses, is a tsunami for me. Sometimes I have to walk away for months. The reality is I wish with all my heart I could win lotteries and run a sanctuary."

"I just try to help these souls," said Robin, a retired accountant who started networking in 2013 from her home in rural Alabama. In 2017, she began posting on Facebook as "Arabian Kill Pen and Auction Horse Group" and "The Arabian 300 Club." That's where we met, horse-loving strangers clicking back and forth online.

Robin and her allies focus on Arabians that are often dumped at auction in entire herds. Often owners pass away without plans for their horses or get too old, too frail, or too broke to care for them. Between 2016 and 2019, Robin posted and phoned twelve to fourteen hours a day; in that time, she and her friends helped place 2,205 otherwise doomed horses.

"I only know one guy that contributes," she explained. "We are 98 percent female. We come from all over, and gosh, a lot of them come from one profession: nursing."

Why, I asked her, why the big gap between the sexes when it comes to caring and acting for equines?

"Men have to have a purpose and a reason to act, whereas if anything needs to be taken care of, women want to nurture it," Robin answered. "We are used to taking care, especially older women like myself."

Robin's passion for horses bloomed in her Texas childhood, where she was de facto an only child, since her sisters were thirteen and eighteen years older.

"When I was little, I'd throw coins in every fountain and make a wish for a horse," she told me (something I had done as well). "And I wanted to go to schools where they learn how to jump."

She worked in accounting for forty years, then in computer science and also earned a degree in information technology. Like many rescuers, some fosters are failures: the rescuer keeps the horse herself. So it is with Robin.

"I have seven horses here, and five are worthless, but don't tell 'em I said that," Robin confessed. "Most of them are old. My mare is thirty-two, and the rest are in their late twenties."

"You have to really be a Chamber of Commerce type with people who want to rescue a horse," she explained. "A lot of them never rescued before, and they have not a clue about transport, quarantine, or anything. You gotta teach new ones the same things over and over again. You've got people who want to home a horse but don't know how to do it. I write instructions for them, but people don't read. 'Why do they need quarantine?' they ask me. And we need more people doing this because those who rescue get full."

To my surprise, I learned that Robin and other rescue networkers face vigorous opposition, even online sabotage, from people who oppose rescue. This group (again, many women) point out that kill buyers just buy more horses with the sales they make to rescuers. Some of them successfully lobbied Facebook to block posting animals for sale. Now equine rescues post carrot icons instead of dollar figures or direct viewers to their pages to use private messages to learn the price of a horse in peril.

"Those people are nuts," Robin said. "Do they not understand if a horse is for sale, and if they don't get purchased by a home, that horse is gonna go for meat? Every horse has a value, even for its meat and bones."

So she wields her Chamber of Commerce charms on the kill buyers, keeping her tone warm and her requests cordial, anything to buy more time for an imperiled horse, to get a horse to a good home.

In the world of rescuers versus meat men, how do you think the latter reconcile the misery they cause, I wonder.

"They don't think about it, it's all they've known and grew up with," Robin tells me. "Mike McBarron runs a kill buying business in Forney, Texas, and he told me 'Robin, if I quit buyin' and sellin' horses, I don't know what I would do. I've been doing this since a child, it's all I know.'"

Even in the horse auction industry, there is a gender difference, she notes. "Women are more the horse dealers; they don't think about buying and selling them by the pound."

Perhaps rescuers are driven by an enhanced sense of responsibility, I suggest.

"Absolutely, you won't network horses if you don't have it," she answers. "Yes, we are bleeding hearts. We take the responsibility to try to do our best to home them."

Robin coordinates rescue via phones and computer now five hours day, and there is no end to the stream of horses, ponies and other equines in crisis. It takes a toll on her, as it does with all rescuers.

"It's emotional burnout more than anything," Robin tells me. "I'm not as nice and enthusiastic as I used to be, and you have to be really upbeat. You have to have a smile on your face when you work for the Chamber, and that's true of rescue, too. Not only are they your customers but also your support group, so these people are very important, and you've gotta be nice to 'em."

Lately, she has turned the work over to friends, especially to Terra Rayoff, a tax preparer in Michigan. Terra's Stone Valley's Ray of Hope Equine Rescue has 12,000 online followers/members, Terra said, although only about 300 donate. Working the net and phones, Terra and Robin reached out to donors, adopters and transporters to save a total of 4,578 since 2016.

"Ninety-five percent of our donors and probably eighty-five percent of the transporters are female," Terra confirmed to me. "The men that do transport are usually more about the money than the care of the horses. I think rescue is more about heart and passion, something women have more of than men when it comes to animals."

More women are banding together in networks similar to theirs, using internet sites to alert followers about horses in peril, to offer transport, to set up quarantine. Most of the work is horse by horse, but at times there are clusters, even whole herds saved. At a 2021 Colorado auction where a bully of a horsemeat man had had the run of it for years, women raised funds, secured homes and saved thirty-seven of the forty-three horses run through the ring from going to him.

Horse-loving women with computers, phones, and chutzpah are a force to be reckoned with. One August day in 2022, trolling through Facebook horse postings, I spotted a silver seven-year-old Quarter Horse gelding on a kill buyer page in Alabama; his left hind leg was visibly broken. Nonetheless, the yard man was slapping him with a stick and describing him as "reins good." The price of the suffering gelding, named Traveler, was $1,000. Dozens of (mostly female) viewers had the same reaction I did: pure fury. I phoned the police department and the animal shelter in the small town nearest the auction yard, pleading for help. This horse needed euthanasia, and it didn't take a veterinarian to see it. The workday was ending, soon no one would be available.

Facebook was aflame with women who felt a similar rage, and within two hours, one woman had paid his bail, another paid for his euthanasia, and the posting for Traveler was removed from the page.

"I am not a freaking hero," Penny Parker insists, yet she estimates she has saved four thousand or more horses from slaughter. To fund her Horse Angel's Rescue/Sharing and Caring Group, she does horse transport, and she is driving a truck and horse trailer from New York to Maine when I catch her.

"I was an optician for thirty years, then ten years ago I quit my job to do this full time," she tells me. "I work twenty-four hours a day. I've aged. I'm just exhausted. But I am happy. This is what I wanted to do all my life—have a field of rescue horses."

The fields of Penny's dreams are an equine rescue and sanctuary in West Chester, Pennsylvania, and rehabilitation barns in Oxford, Pennsylvania, and Elkton, Maryland. She tells me that 170 horses are spread among them, some for adoption, some unadoptable and therefore in permanent sanctuary. She claims some 24,000 followers on her Facebook page. Her most urgent pleas for help (those written from the heart along with disturbing photos) reach 2,000 to 5,000.

Who does this? Who responds? Who writes "sharing and praying" on her page?

"It is definitely mostly women in the rescue world—maybe 85 percent," she says. "I don't know if as many men have the capability to deal with all the drama in horsepeople and the things that come with it. It takes empathy, passion, determination. You have to be very strong-willed and be able to be tough-skinned. Sleep and food and things people do on a normal daily basis—you go without those. You have to be able to sacrifice."

"When I was three, I used to draw horses all over the place," she tells me, relating classic early onset symptoms. "I was in Brownies and Girl Scouts, my mom was our troop leader, and I'd beg her to take us to the state park where they had a riding facility. I was obsessed. As a teen, I was still drawing horses all over the place. A shrink told my mother I was 'promiscuous,' because I drew horses. Now I've never worked so hard in my life, but I'm doing what I love."

Horses are often saved with only minutes to spare: Titan, a palomino gelding blinded in one eye by his owner with a bullwhip, was dumped into the Bowie, Texas, kill buyer pen and going for $1,200 or being shipped to Mexico in twenty-four-hours. Kat Young and Shelby Sinnett used Messenger and appealed to Maggie, Joanna, Katherine, Janet and others. With three minutes left to keep him off the truck, they raised it.

Susan Kayne is director of the Unbridled Thoroughbred Foundation (UTF), a New York organization that rescues and places off-the-track Thoroughbreds (OTTBs) and advocates for legislation to protect them from slaughter. According to UTF, 7,500 to 18,000 Thoroughbreds are killed annually in slaughter plants. In 2021, Susan and other advocates successfully lobbied the New York State Legislature to pass a bill that prohibits the sale or transfer of New York's Thoroughbred and Standardbred racing or breeding stock for slaughter. Prior to starting Unbridled in 2004, she was a show jumper and galloped (exercised) race horses.

Her TV series, *Unbridled*, earned multiple Telly Awards and the US Equestrian Federation Pegasus Award for Broadcast Media Excellence. Her insider experience helped expose the abuse of performance drugs in race horses featured in a 2012 *New York Times* page one story.

She's one of the most effective, well-known rescuers, and she is not alone. "This really is about 85 percent women," she confirmed when we spoke. "We have men who are generous donors and involved, but they are definitely in the minority. Men who are involved with horses view it more as a business. They are not so attached emotionally to animals. That's the simplest answer as to why it's more women: We are more feeling toward them."

As for feeling, it's all she can do to keep her composure at the auctions where the kill buyers are thick on the ground such as the sales at New Holland, Pennsylvania, and Unadilla, New York.

"The most challenging aspect of rescue for me is I can look at a horse and truly understand what they are feeling," Susan told me. "It is gutting and heart-wrenching to go to auctions. The horses are truly terrified, and there is a subculture of humans who traffic in horses—racehorses, workhorses, camp horses and old horses—beyond anything I've experienced. The hardness and callousness of the people who deal, who put on the auctions, who transport horses from one side of the country to the other in aluminum trailers with no floor mats (horses fall and are trampled), who bring horses who have been together for 10 or 20 years into the sale ring and rip them apart. They have no soul.

"I come from the racing world and know many men trainers, owners and breeders, and many have said to me this is about bottom line," she explained. "Not all are like that by any means: Last weekend (when forty-four Thoroughbreds put up for auction in Unadilla were saved from the meat men) we were empowered by a coalition led by a gentleman who is a trainer."

I tell Susan how, when I was ten or so, my father took me to a small local auction; as I watched the horses and ponies ridden or led into the ring, I felt their fear and saw their confusion. I began to sob. Dad took me home. It was forty years before I attended another horse auction.

Susan must attend them regularly.

Soon both of us are sniffling at our memories.

"I believe all living beings are connected," said Susan. "When we are young, our souls are very open to animals as our friends. As fellow sentient beings, the bond is formed early. What I have observed and experienced is that some can become hardened and callous by what you need to do to survive in the horse business in any discipline. You lose that softness toward the horse."

"I've asked men in racing, 'If there was no prize money at stake would you still do this? Do you love horses or how they make you feel, or the money from it?' This has been followed by long silences. I have not gotten an accurate answer from anyone. There are differing definitions of love, of course, but we rescue horses with no agenda. We believe they all have inherent worth and intrinsic value."

We compare horses we own personally. My OTTB gelding Mine Too turns out to be her mare Possession's half-brother. Both are bright and beautiful chestnuts; however, where "Tooey" was a gift to me from a client, her "Posey" sold for $2.1 million as a yearling at the Keeneland, Kentucky, auction. Years later, she was rescued from slaughter for $200.

Susan knows the auction, breeding and training world intimately.

"I know how much coverup is going on from the real degree of carnage," she told me. "They are brought into this world to serve, then they are abused by morally reprehensible breeders and owners. It is like sex trafficking, the horses are emotionally traumatized. I understand the implications of the word. I am a convert to Judaism, and I say that what's happening is a horse holocaust.

"When I came to understand the capacity and depth of horses as our friends, companions, and fellow sentient beings, I began to question what we are doing and why, and examine my own soul concerning the answers," she said. "That paradigm shift inside me brought me back full circle to genuine, euphoric, unadulterated love for another living being that is different in shape and size and doesn't speak our language, but our hearts speak to one another."

And our mutual and widespread horse craziness? Why so many girls, why so early? Why so powerfully? Why so enduring? I asked her.

"I truly believe it is from birth," Susan told me. "When I was about four, I was lying on the living room floor of the family home and watching our huge old Magnavox TV. I saw Canonero II win the Kentucky Derby—he ran right into my heart. Since then, it has been a long, arduous, exciting journey to bring my own true love of the horse for the horse's sake, not because of anything they can do. Horses chose me."

And me. And millions of us. Can we stop trying to rescue them?

If rescuing eats your life and funds, not rescuing eats your conscience.

So I rescued. Despite Kris' admonishment—and now, in a karmic twist, she has a horsegirl daughter—I rescue.

After watching thousands of horses online, one day while scrolling through the dreaded Bastrop, Louisiana, kill pen site, I spotted a video clip of a small, dark brown Morab (Morgan and Arabian) gelding. His huge dark eyes, shapely compact body, quick forward trot did it. In those seconds, lightning struck me. Here were my two favorite breeds in one molasses-colored package, going cheap or shipping to slaughter.

I called my friend Laurie, who called her friend Amy. We had little time. If they are even lucky enough to be listed publicly, horses in slaughter pens have very few days, sometimes just hours, to be purchased from the kill buyer. Amy provided the funds to purchase the gelding (about $750), then the fees to board him for the required two-week quarantine and ship him north to us. Laurie and I provided care, tack, experience, and most handling and riding.

Although Amy christened our sleek brown boy Dusty, he is so indisputably handsome that I call him Darcy (as in Mr. Darcy of Jane Austen fame) and so charming that I added "Darling." Dusty Darcy Darling settled in, never getting a nick or kick from other horses, always finding a friend or three, ever willing to be groomed, ridden, kissed on the nose and included in discussions when we stand around the yard. He knows cues, and he parks out (stretching his forelegs and hindlegs) as show horses in the Morgan and Saddlebred world do. He has clearly been a driving horse as well. I ran lines through my stirrups and ground drove him: he listened, he turned quickly and lightly to "gee" (right) and "haw" (left) and understood "back."

The more I ride him, meanwhile, the better we dance.

Darcy is a horse I sit into, not on. I meld with him as if I were a pole through a carousel horse, and we zoom, bend and tear off, sure of each other. It's a sensation I knew with my previous Arabians; I have no sense of coming loose in the saddle (he's too round, wither-less and slick to ride bareback). When we plunge through a field of restored prairie, he snatches at the tips of big bluestem that reach above my shoulder. When we pause, he turns his head and peeks back at me, hoping for a morsel for standing still.

"You smarty pants little bugger!" I tell him. "You don't get a cookie for everything you do." He accepts this with good cheer, and we trot away into the pines and birches.

Most of all, I adore him: his expressive eyes, his quality of what horse people call "dryness," his plump butt, his small ears, the flair of his nostrils, the fine wrinkles at his throat—exactly the wrinkles of the horses that prance in The Elgin Marbles that once adorned the Parthenon above Athens.

In partnerships like this, my legs become his legs and feet, my eyes and ears are his. I sense the ground—slick grass or yielding soil, hardpacked or giving—through his hooves. I sense his eyes flickering at the light on a huge ivory puffball among the oak leaves, the shadow in the hazel bush, his ears at the waves sifting the sand at the lake's edge. We are, for this while, a centaur.

Knowing horses, knowing who they are, the pleasure they give and what befalls them if no one cares, there is no choice for me: get a pedicure or donate that amount to a horse rescue? There is no "or," so my nails go unkempt, and the price of that is clicked toward a thrown-away Thoroughbred, a draft horse with painful, neglected hooves and ribs like the spars of a shipwreck, a pregnant Fjord mare, a one-eyed Appaloosa, a donkey whose hide would otherwise become "medicine" in China.

As my college reunion approached, I was repeatedly asked to donate to the college fund. Instead of a suitably significant gift for the suitably significant year, I wrote a letter to the alumni office: "Horses have no multimillion-dollar investment portfolio to protect them. So my gift will go to them."

To the annoyance of friends that I tag on Facebook without mercy, I help because I feel I can and should. And also because I am on the receiving end of rescuing, which animals can do like nothing else.

When I can't take it, whatever it is—vile self-serving politicians, the news of the proceeding eco-apocalypse, the death of a horse at the racetrack, dogs barbecued in Asia, the onslaught of need in a parent that cannot ever be met—then I ride. It is the balm, the poultice of the body and spirit, and it begins immediately.

Fetching Darcy from the pasture, I pass two young sandhill cranes, their plumage the buckskin color of local deer. I hear the Gglup! Errrk! of pond frogs. We jump a few logs and splash into the pond to see if the water plants are still tasty. From there I watch herons and observe pairs of mallards. I pose myself an intermittent dare: Are we ready for that coop or will he run out and take me under the low-hanging elm branch?

I dismount to tip a bluebird house back to vertical, hark to a wren scold as a loon calls from one end of the lake to another. On level ground, I sit the trot, gently asking him to please lower his head, lift his back, throw his weight to his hindquarters. He snakes his neck, tosses his nose, and dances defiance.

Two hours afterward, I am driving home as dried sweat cools on my scalp. I check for ticks every few minutes, running my fingers up my neck, behind my ears, under my T-shirt. I pluck a pale green inch worm from my hair. There is half a carrot inside my breeches behind my right knee. These breeches have no pockets, and I had tucked it in my waistband and forgotten.

For these hours, I have not had to be tactful, tactical, thoughtful, accountable or compliant. I have not had to act "Chamber of Commerce-y" to get things done. I have not had to slow down or hurry up for anyone or listen to anyone but the horse beneath me, and he, when he feels like it, listens to me.

I hear no don'ts, just do's from deep inside.

I have, for this while, myself been rescued.

CHAPTER 16

Galloping Scotland

"These days, of course, it's mostly girls that are horse-struck. Boys can take horses or leave them, but with girls it's as if the teenage Elizabeth Taylor in National Velvet were part of their gene pool."

~Michael Korda, *Horse People*

"Tits and teeth, ladies! Tits and teeth!" Jane called to us over the clatter of eight-hundred hooves on cobblestone, over the cheers of children and adults, over the barking dogs and the flap of blue and yellow banners from windows. Jane set the example, her teeth flashing below glossy russet bangs and pink cheeks under her hunt cap, her bosom thrust forward in her form-fitting tweed jacket.

In the wake of the television series *Outlander*, female tourists now flock to Scotland in search of men, specifically That Man. That was not why I was trotting next to Jane on my own redhead, Kingston, a confident chestnut gelding with legs like elephant trunks and a brontosaurus-size neck set off with a perfectly braided mane.

It had been going on three years of Covid restrictions and I was whirling around in my own exhaust fumes on the quest for the essence of horsegirldom. I decided I could continue to stay home drinking sauvignon blanc, re-watching *Outlander* star Sam Heughan, and wiping cat hair off the bathroom floor tiles, or I could live.

I combined two passions and bought a riding vacation on the Scottish border, a challenge for advanced riders only, jubilantly described by the Australian women who run the company as "raucous" and "fast-paced." I paid for it in installments and packed my boots, helmet and breeches.

On this trip, I decided I would not interview, I would not scrutinize, I would not pose the usual questions about background, birth order, age of onset, etc. I would savor Scotland, ride the horses, drink the whiskey, and just appreciate living and breathing. And riding, of course.

So I sallied off to Scotland for the horses in what's known as Riding the Marches or the Common Riding.

Since the fourteenth century, locals on the borders with England have galloped the boundaries of their burghs to defend them from reivers (livestock thieves). The annual re-enactments have been males-only events (with a tiny handful of exceptions in the early twentieth century) for reasons spurious and mostly involving singing and drinking between rides. This policy was defended with statements such as "it's aye been so"—which, I concede, delivered in a Scots accent, is beguiling if irrational. Local women even prevented other women from riding as in 1996 when they formed a human barricade on High Street in the mill town of Hawick. Still other women went to court to get the right to ride in the events and won.

I'd heard about all this in New Zealand while riding with a Scot who returned home each year to take part. I decided I wasn't about to stay home and seethe with envy while the "braw laddies" had all the fun.

We happy few were to take part in a week of "rideouts" based in Hawick (perversely pronounced "hoik") leading up to a re-enactment of a young Scot (the Cornet) and the callants (his three male attendants) leading hundreds of riders through town carrying the village pennant in a ceremony honoring the stealing of a pennant from the occupying British in 1514.

In nearby Cringletie House, our country mansion hotel near Peebles, I met the other riders: Angela, a psychologist, and Tessa, a prison guard, both from Holland; Kristin, executive director of a non-profit group; Elise, an Indiana veterinary clinic receptionist; Jane, who had worked with people with dementia issues, and Julie, a retired general practitioner, both from Lancashire; Shannon, a chemical engineer, arrived from California with her non-riding husband, Jim. I was the oldest by far. The youngest of us was Ann, a Texas political organizer, whose non-riding boyfriend, Justin, photo documented, brought flowers, held horses, shuttled us to ride launches, helped set up the lunch tents, and toted our various bags so amiably that I dubbed him "Prince Consort."

Suzie McIntosh at Kailzie Equestrian Centre provided the horses: Irish drafts or Irish draft crosses with powerful haunches and legs, steady minds and tireless lungs. Several things happened the first day when we went for a brisk hack (trail ride) led by Kailzie's Chief of Staff Gemma, to test our horses: nearly everyone began to fall in love with her mount. Then we each began to compare and question what we owned and rode at home.

"I want one of these! Do you think Suzie would sell him/her? What do you think it costs to import one?" became the refrain. Schemes began to hatch of buying Suzie's horses, which are sold at rare times and in tiny numbers, with first choice going to the British royal military escorts and to police. Our love affairs grew over the week during the rides themselves. Tessa with big bay Socrates, Elise with Leros, Kristina with Acropolis, and Julie and all of us with Bruno, a chestnut with a choir boy expression and long legs.

On the mornings of the rideouts themselves, we mounted up in a parking lot on the Tweed River and melded into the hundreds of riders streaming through the village center. We queen-waved our way up the road to applause and cheers.

"Hooray!" went the red-nosed men outside the pubs.

"Hooray!" went the old woman from her balcony.

"Hooray!" went the father and son from the doorway of the curry and kebab shop.

"Hooray, hurrah!" went the families on the sidewalks, people spilling into the gutters, more people lining driveways up the hill and into the countryside. The Cornet and his men hit the first pasture, and the whole body of us charged forward in a mad gallop—the first of hours to come.

This was not your nice little haunches-under, elevated-forehand, nose-near-the-vertical, nicely-on-the-bit canter. All of Scotland's border country lay before us, and the horses and local riders knew it.

This was the Charge of the Light Brigade minus artillery. It was pell-mell pelting straight up hills and down again with no half-halts, much less halts. The horses were keen, we were all stuck tight to our saddles, heels down and eyes half-blinded with tears from the wind, the speed, and joy.

Tessa, chief extrovert of the group, gave a few "woooo-hooos!" and headed her bay gelding for the male foursome at the front of the whole cavalcade. Angela, Ann, Julie, Jane, Shannon, Elise, Kristin and I were not far behind her.

I'd asked for a forward horse, and Susie had given me one in Kingston.

"Good boy, Kingston," I breathed, as we thundered up the sheep pastures to the tops and down through slatey fields and up again to views over vast pine plantings, then whipped down a slope, skirting a loch where a sign warned "Beware of Adders in This Loch."

"Good boy, Kingston!" I gasped as we jumped unseen ditches grooved into the hills, clattered through streets, plashed across streams, clopped over stone bridges and back into forest lanes shaded with monster oaks, lime trees, rowan, and hawthorn.

Kingston loved keeping up as close as possible to the front of the horde with his friends, so that whenever I looked back, the line of riders ran far into the distance, its end never in sight.

I told him "Good boy, Kingston!" as he skirted a hidden bog that sucked two of the callants down to their boot tops and slammed their horses to a stop. I thanked Kingston all the way through every ride, standing up in my stirrups to get off his back, bridging my reins to stay off his mouth, and never needing to "kick on" because he took charge and led just as a good dance partner does. Tessa, Jane, Julie, Angela and everyone else stayed with me, stayed on, and stayed astonished at our speed, waving to each other and hooting with glee. Deep in this throng of mostly young-to-middle-aged male riders (the oldest was Charlie Muir, a 72-year-old retired rugby referee), Tessa managed to flirt as well as hoot.

At home in Minnesota, I have a growing number of friends who are appalled that I go to other states and other countries to ride horses not my own. It's so inconceivable to some that they assume I fly or drive my own horse there. More and more of them confine their riding to indoor and outdoor arenas and familiar level, dry trails, and always on their own horse, year after year. They are strictly monogamous, and they look at me as if I am committing blatant infidelity or, at the very least, sure to get killed.

"Don't ride with Karin," my friends Ernie and Marilyn, owners of a nearby stable, caution new boarders. "She goes fast."

Fast? I had slowed to mostly trots and tiny bits of canter for those folks. Nonetheless, I was not subsequently invited to join their stately parades around the hayfield.

So it was without any qualms that I went to Scotland, that I climbed onto whatever horse Suzie provided. I didn't even think about it. I trust that whatever I hire, whatever is loaned to me, if they have brakes and are honest to jumps, I can get aboard, check my girth, adjust my stirrups, and in less than ten minutes' acquaintance, it's over the hills and walls and perhaps the dreaded ditches. It had worked for me in Ireland, Canada, New Zealand and around the U.S. I had been confident it would work in Scotland.

Here above the Tweed River, among the lambs and ewes, Julie, Jane, Kristin, Tessa, Elise, Ann, Angela and Shannon plainly had the same attitude. Not one of us fell off or even came close to it. We stayed in our saddles and savored it all, with occasional boosts of whiskey from our newly bought flasks during the rare and brief pauses.

Of course I had to ask the questions: Why so many women on this and other riding trips? Why so many girls and women owning, rescuing, loving horses?

"I feel like men ride as a hobby or a profession," said Elise, the rider from Indiana. "Women ride as a passion. It's in our blood."

At the end of the day, back at Suzie's huge lorry, a swarm of slim teen and pre-teen girls glided forward to take the reins, untack our horses and load them into the lorry where hay nets awaited. Hawick is legendary for its whiskey and cashmere, but stores were closed by this hour, so we tromped off to the Drumlanrig pub. There I found yet another horsewoman: Ashley, the owner, had galloped racehorses at the track as a teen. She now worked in the bar when she was not practicing mounted archery in Qatar where her fireman husband worked on oil rigs.

Day after day, it was not all horseback fun, it was also games. I looked out the window at Cringletie one morning to see two men in kilts (aye!) setting up archery, small cabers and stones for miniature versions of the Highland games. They also placed boots for "Wellie wangin'" (throwing Wellington boots into hoops) and lastly, balls and a prime bottle as a target for the Haggis Malt Challenge.

"Piss off!" yelled Julie as she launched her caber successfully onto guidelines pinned into the lawn. The most petite of our group, she kept up at all times, and no one would have known about her recurrent cancer, had she not told someone, who whispered to the rest.

"I can always tell my horse people patients," Julie told us. "They don't moan." She certainly did not. And over the days, we didn't, despite intermittent rain showers, hours of fast riding, occasional wind, unseen chafing, and no potty stops.

That the vast majority of the riders on common riding days were men intrigued me. The only other place I'd seen this turnout of males on horseback was on trips to Ireland, the historic epicenter of the horse world. I'd been there once for lessons in cross country riding at Clonshire Equestrian Centre just outside the picturesque village of Adare in County Limerick. I was writing feature stories for an equestrian magazine, and squeezed in a trip to the legendary Dublin Horse Show, too.

If anatomy is to some extent destiny in athletics, women would dominate riding sports, since there are no fragile external organs in areas where they can get mashed. When it comes to staying in the middle of the horse, women also have the benefit of a lower center of gravity and a more mobile pelvis, a big advantage for all that sitting trot in dressage just as it is for the high speed turns in barrel racing.

However, in Ireland, for reasons I wanted to know, boys and men still participate in great numbers in horse sports. So while I was attempting the Common Ridings in Scotland, I put in a call over the water to Sue Foley, who runs Clonshire.

"It's different here in some ways," noted Sue. "We have a good amount of boys and men that ride in Ireland. It's considered quite a macho sport here. In the riding schools and in training for exams and qualifications there are definitely less men, but professionally all our international team members in eventing and showjumping are men, and the dressage team is all girls."

What did Sue see in her classes that might highlight differences in the ways Irish youngsters approach riding, I asked.

"We are conscious in Clonshire to make the lessons varied and interesting or we lose the boys," she explained. "They need more than just riding in circles, and they don't care much about the horse and how he goes. It could be a bike under them—they want the buzz."

Temperament and anatomy, Sue confirmed, play a role in propelling girls and boys into or away from the sport.

"I do feel that women and girls will stick at something longer and will see it out the other end, where boys, if it doesn't work out immediately, will give it up," she said. "They don't want to lose face or be embarrassed if they fail or fall. Also, it hurts their willies, especially when starting off, and I think they won't say it. So after a few lessons, if they can't get the rising (posting) trot, they can't take the pain."

"Men and women compete on level terms in the horse world, and that's nice," Sue said. "Horse racing is big here in Ireland, and the lighter, braver boys head that direction—that's a very male section and a bit rough."

Rough it might be, but Riding the Borders in Scotland, however, was not competitive. There are no winners, just survivors. And my all-female band survived, joyfully, and celebrated it every evening.

One evening at our digs at Cringletie House, a piper appeared in the salon, six feet tall plus the requisite black ostrich feather bonnet. With Highland cattle browsing the slope behind him through the muntined windows, John Connor explained about "war pipes and the fighting machine they are—they will make you fight anybody, even shadows." Before he recited Robert Burns' "Address to a Haggis," he did indeed play "Over the Sea to Skye," better known now as the theme from *Outlander.*

Yes, we were all falling in love, helplessly and permanently with Scotland (Ann and Justin immediately popped online to scout a possible home to purchase). And instantly and forever with our mounts. Jamie Fraser would have to wait. We were riding!

If a piper were not romance enough, there was the ocean gallop.

One day, Suzie packed our horses in the lorry to nearby Dunbar on the coast of the Firth of Forth, part of the North Sea. We walked the horses quietly onto the John Muir Country Park shoreline, then let them rip on the deserted beach. No brakes, again, and by this time none of us wanted them.

It was thunder on the sand with Gemma on a huge gray gelding ahead of us, swiveling in her saddle to shoot photos. Tessa dropped her reins and mugged for Justin's camera, Jane urged her heavy gelding on, Julie sat gleeful and tight on Bruno, and I kept my head steady in the spray for the benefit of my helmet camera. We went up the beach, turned, went down the beach, more of us into the surf, then up again before walking, happily salted—both horses and women—back the final time. We had lived a cliché, a dream gallop, and it proved to be bliss.

"I'm not technically a good horsewoman," Jane said to us at dinner that night, "but I can't imagine life without horses. What do people do who don't ride?"

Shannon's husband Jim, we learned, had run more than 50 marathons, so there was one answer.

Ann was the last, at the end of our final rideout day, to say goodbye to her mare, Aphrodite. We all drew well back in the riverside parking lot at Hawick to watch our horses—OUR horses—load into the van. And we wept, too, or at least I did, knowing that what had just taken place had bonded us, lifted us, and surely was the ride of a lifetime. I pushed it back temporarily by footing it over to the pub to drink Guinness among the men in dirty riding boots and sweaty breeches with the roar of soccer games on the pub's TV.

"Ah, you were a wild one, weren't ya?" a sodden and besotted enthusiast two-thirds my age, wearing the standard yellow cashmere vest of the callants, kept gurgling at me. After about his third gurgle and a couple of pats on my knee, I moved. I overlooked the insulting use of the past tense and scuttled over to hide between Justin and Ann.

The following morning, following the usual hearty breakfast (steel cut oatmeal bathed in cream and whiskey was my favorite) we left Cringletie with tears, hugs, and ardent promises to meet somewhere, somehow and surely with horses again. I squeezed into the rental car, and Tessa and Elise carried me the too-brief route to Edinburgh.

A day later, I flew to Norway where I bunked with old friends in a fisherman's cottage renovated to bright snugness overlooking the blue and green water of a fjord. Were horses over for now? How would I get my daily fix or was it the DTs for me?

On a cool morning on a hillside above the fjord, I joined my friends to watch a local sport club. There were sprints for toddlers, slightly longer runs for older children, and a half-marathon on a twisting trail that ran from where apple juice and hot dogs wrapped in lefse were served up the hills through the pines, boulders and birches and back.

And then I saw her, her blond hair in a ponytail, her tall socks pulled up over her breeches to the suede knee patches. Her mother was already off with one of her younger sisters in the half-marathon. I had to return to my quest, I had to ask:

"What's your name?"

"Lise Marit."

"How old are you?"

"Sixteen."

"What do you ride?"

"A twenty-year-old Norwegian warmblood."

And that was enough.

We are everywhere. We are everywhere.

CHAPTER 17

Mongol Derby

"One strand of Mongolian philosophy has it that my chest, not my brain, is the seat of my consciousness. It contains my hiimori, my wind-horse, an inner creature whose power needs maintaining.

When you rub a racehorse's sweat into your forehead or ride a great, quick pony, you strengthen your hiimori and improve your destiny."

~Lara Prior-Palmer,
Rough Magic: Riding the World's Loneliest Horse Race

Even from the air, I spot the signs far below: The tawny-gold raked footing of dressage stables; the pale-gray raked footing for jumping stables, and the living hedgerows inset with wooden coops and rails for hunters. Just outside Washington, D.C., lies big-time horse country, and down among the paddocks, run-in sheds, and windbreaks is the toughest female rider I know.

The woman I am flying to visit is a rider of the most extreme kind. This is not just my opinion: The Mongol Derby, initiated in 2009, is featured in the *Guinness Book of World Records* as the world's longest and toughest horse race.

In August 2018, Carol Federighi of Takoma, Maryland, completed the 1,000-kilometer (621-mile) race, galloping over the steppes on twenty-two small and not terribly well-broken horses over a maximum time of ten days. At the time, it was the capstone of a pastime of competing in endurance rides of fifty, a hundred miles or more. What propels her? I am keen to know.

This derby is no two-minute track event, no sunny day betting frenzy and fashion show lubricated by mint juleps. It is a re-run of the postal messenger route established by Genghis Khan in the thirteenth century that covered his empire. Riders are limited to a saddle pack with a sleeping bag and clothes totaling five kilograms. Riders describe it as "epic horses" "the closest thing to flying" "amazing and absolutely terrifying but still the best feeling on Earth! It's a feeling like no other flying over the steppe on those strong horses."

There is no exaggerating the difficulty, danger and demands on the rider's body.

In 2013, 19-year-old Lara Prior-Palmer of Great Britain was warned by a previous competitor that it involved "broken ribs, amputated fingers, cracked pelvises, punctured lungs, torn ligaments, broken collarbones…bucking ponies, fraying girths, sicknesses, extreme dehydration, getting lost, not fun, don't expect fun." She entered anyway and became the youngest person and first female to win it.

More women enter each year, Carol among them.

About half the starting riders make it to the finish line, and Carol outlasted many of the forty-four competitors from twelve countries.

"I can see you doing that, Karin," friends tell me, when I let them know about my mission to meet Carol.

Nope. Not even one day, probably not even an hour or so, thanks. I do, however, want to know what makes this horse-loving woman, one of the truly impressive of an above-average tough cohort, tick.

Is her attraction the physical risk and rigor? The mental challenges? Is it self-mastery or fellowship or the horses? Or is it something else?

It is August, and when I arrive to meet her, Maryland and D.C. swelter in jungle-like humidity. Tiger swallowtails flutter and loop amid honeysuckle vines, strangler vines as big as a man's arm embrace trees, bamboo thickets and incongruous holly trees mix with magnolias and mighty water oaks among the lawns, slopes and ravines. I drive my rental car past a sign that says Rock Creek Stables, and the heat has made me so deeply and abruptly stupid that it takes a beat before I realize that's where Carol and I will be riding.

The prospect of pounding along in this cauldron on 900 pounds of very fit, heat-radiating Arabian has little appeal except in the abstract. Yet I really want to know how and why she does this. And I want to meet her horses, of course, those she uses for her numerous U.S. endurance ride competitions.

Just up the slope from the parched and shrinking streambed of Sligo Creek, Carol and her husband, Brian Coss, are renovating a modern one-story home. Carol greets me in their driveway. Tall, with pale skin, thick red-gold hair to her shoulders, and a typical horsewoman's absence of makeup, she hasn't an extra ounce on her frame. My impression of her is not one of thinness but of quiet, wiry strength.

A stationary bike occupies their home office where the horse literature canon—Jane Smiley, Michael Korda, Sally Swift—perches on crowded bookshelves above an acrylic case of trophy belt buckles from endurance wins.

"Carol has eighty percent of those—she doesn't quit very often," says Brian, a trim man with a goatee wearing riding breeches. It's auspicious that Brian is also a rider and a good one. He's an attorney, retired from the Department of Justice, where Carol, also an attorney, still works.

Their engagement photo adorns one of the shelves: Brian, bearing a bouquet of red roses, looks ardently at Carol, who offers a rose to a gray Arabian (their gelding, Stetson) cuddled close to her shoulder. This is what it truly is to marry a horsegirl, I think. It will be at least a threesome.

Carol and Brian first met when he offered her a bottle of cold water during an endurance riding clinic. Since then, they have merged their domestic lives and their herds: Her former eventing horse, a Quarter Horse named Gobi, is retired to the country along with two elderly Arabians: Piper and Miss Chriss. Their two current endurance horses are fifteen minutes' drive away at those Rock Creek Stables, a 1,700-acre preserve in the heart of D.C.

Endurance rides of twenty-five, fifty, seventy-five and one hundred miles are conducted in the U.S. under the auspices of the American Endurance Ride Conference (AERC). The mother of them all is the Tevis Cup in Auburn, California, which takes place over a hundred miles in twenty-four hours during a full summer moon. It features a 18,000-foot ascent, a 22,000-foot descent and a vicious steep area called Cougar Rock. Where it is especially sheer, the young athletic people and runners dismount and run alongside their horse.

When Tevis began in 1954, it was acknowledged as the toughest test of horse and rider in the world. As recently as 2022, horses have died in this race.

That was before the Mongol Derby launched in 2008 followed by the Gaucho Derby in Patagonia in 2018. (The endurance race in the film *Hidalgo* is fictitious, by the way. But star Viggo Mortensen can *really* ride.)

AERC rides are timed events with horses subject to periodic veterinary checks. Riders whose horses fail the checks due to dehydration, lameness, high heart rates, etc., are pulled from the race. It's a test of ability and fitness, soundness and heart, which few breeds other than the Arabian can handle.

"Arabians are the most competitive and easiest to get through, because they cool down quickly while other horses are skating along the edge," Carol tells me. "So Arabians predominate, although these rides are open to all horse breeds as well as mules."

"Endurance racing is a sport of having the right stuff where you need it, spread out over miles and miles," says Carol, whose accumulated AERC race mileage is approaching 3,000 miles when we meet. At a typical race of one hundred miles, she will have five bags of food, water and horse gear to plan and organize. "If you have a crew, they organize the bags and travel from stop to stop. It takes manpower or organizational skills."

"It's a matter of a high level of organization from Carol," Brian confirms, approvingly.

In their spare bedroom, I change to boots and breeches, then Carol and I head to Rock Creek Horse Center. Nancy Reagan rode there, and a plaque near the office commemorates her support of its therapeutic riding program. Half the fifty-five horses and ponies here are owned by the National Park Service, and twenty-some are privately owned, Brian being one of only three male boarders.

In a corner box stall, I meet Stetson, a twenty-year-old gray gelding whose black muzzle and dark eyes are enhanced with pink speckles, a rare de-pigmentation carried in some Arabian genes. Down the aisle a few stalls is Bakari, an eleven-year-old chestnut mare with a dreamy long mane wafting over her glossy shoulders. They are both Shagyas, a Hungarian strain of Arabian reputed to be less high strung than others. In the absence of cavalry wars to fight, they are now excelling at endurance racing.

Twilight falls in the park as we head out, Carol on her mare, me on Stetson. They wear bitless bridles and slip-on protective boots over their unshod hooves. I discover my treeless saddle and wide stirrups are a treat, far more supportive than classic stirrups and the firm trees of Western or English saddles. I find I sit comfortably on Stetson's back with no rubbing or restrictions for either of us. He is steady, he listens, he trots on and reins back just as I ask. He is never rude, but he also doesn't give a damn about me—he has a job to do!

We pass under immensely tall tulip poplars and straight beeches—who knew D.C. had such an old forest smack in its middle? From the creepers, briars and ivy there is a constant undertone of clicking insects. Fireflies rise lugubriously, winking at half speed against the dark bank on our left. The shallow creek glitters past on the right, trickling almost silently in the fading light.

When I spoke with Carol, I learned that regular 100-mile rides were not enough for her: in Virginia in 2018, she entered the Old Dominion Hundred in a category called "Cavalry" in which riders agree to get no help and carry everything with them, including horse feed, except water.

"I entered for the challenge of it, and because it simplifies life," Carol says. "You don't need bags or other people. You have everything right with you. I tried it once, and my horse was just too slow. I want to try that one again."

This is a subspecies of horsegirl, I think, with admiration. And I am not of this subspecies.

As a teenager, I did a 20-mile trotting race (all kids in Western saddles) and found it boring and hot that morning and even more boring and hot as the day slogged into afternoon. My Arabian gelding, Gabe, took it in the proverbial Arabian stride, barely breaking a sweat. I, however, resolved: never again!

Before she met Brian, Carol enrolled in a clinic in Utah with Christopf Schork, a world champion endurance rider. A gymnast, mountain climber, triathlete, bi-athlete, ski instructor, mountain biker, rower, kayaker, etc., Schork, at least on paper, has a certain terrifying intensity, perhaps typical of endurance sports athletes, including Carol and Brian.

Brian's sport for a quarter century was flying planes. Once retired, he returned to riding, which seems to be much of the mucilage of their marriage. When riding led to endurance riding, he crewed for Schork in order to learn the ropes.

Their couples time includes lots of truck hours. Carol and Brian do some endurance driving to get to these endurance races, trucking themselves, their horses and gear north to Vermont or down to the Carolinas. On one occasion, they crossed the continental U.S., shooting from D.C. to California for the Tevis Cup.

"I like the challenge of putting it all together, getting the horse in condition, and, by implication, yourself," Carol says. "It was our horses, we conditioned and brought them there. At Tevis we finished 17th of the 168 riders that started."

"It is something you can do together, and the trailer, truck and tools appeal to guys," she tells me. So they do, but they also complain about the hard riding, and with good reason. Is it a marriage held together by love of rugged thrills?

What goes on here, I wonder.

Whatever it is, they do it together, although satisfaction, much less pleasure, is never guaranteed. One of their 100-mile races involved a route that was "slippery, dark, hilly, woods, twisty and turn-y and we walked the last 15 miles," she recalls.

In 2019, pounding along in the 100-mile Vermont Challenge in record heat, Brian and Stetson were pulled out of the competition at 62 miles because Stetson showed lameness.

"I'm not sure what leg he was lame on, but at that point he was twenty years old and starting to feel the aches and pains of aging joints, etc.," says Carol, who completed the race on Bakari in twenty-three hours and thirty-eight minutes. To say it was not fun is to understate things.

"It was more grueling than ever—of thirty starters just sixteen finished," she relates, as I am thinking this marriage is founded on a shared love of masochism. "It was only ninety-six degrees but miserable, and I had no crew and no ice, and I was thinking '*Please pull me. Please!*' That kind of heat is normal for a D.C. summer, but it is grueling for Vermont. It felt like our horses were conditioned for the heat but they had to move slowly, so we did. I was telling myself '*I will never do this again.*' I could be home having a cocktail and reading."

Would she have been, though? At the DOJ, Carol practices what she calls "endurance litigation," working on briefs until 4 a.m. on occasion. What would she do if she didn't have her job, I ask.

"I'd probably do more sport more often and be in better shape when I did do it," is her answer. "Being in a high-test job is part of the same personality disorder; it has to be a challenge."

The heat this evening is enough of a challenge for me: Rock Creek's ratio of rocks and boulders to water is about ten to one in this drought. There is enough water, however, for the horses to step in and drink. Bakari declines, but Stetson sips and savors.

"Stetson is the Zen master, you can't get him excited about anything," Carol points out when I compliment him. "He's so good, and at a vet check his heart rate is already down to forty-eight. Bakari is very like a mare: opinionated, things need to be done her way, and you must convince her it is her idea before she will do it. If you kick her, she starts backing up: 'No, no, no! I don't want to run if someone kicks me!' She pretends she's tough and doesn't need people, but she is very snuggly, loves brushing, and stands in a kind of coma when you comb her hair and braid her mane."

Apart from the fitness required from both rider and horse, endurance riding takes mental fortitude. I confess I prefer short, intense rides with gallops and jumps and would not know how to occupy my mind with long trotting rides. There is a difference between stamina, which is physical, and endurance, which is in large part mental, I am learning. What Carol does is a race, I must understand, and not an ultra-long trail ride for some sort of perverse pleasure. She is deadly serious about it. Presumably, this is what all endurance riders are compelled to be for the sake of their horses and themselves.

"There is no chit-chat; you pay attention to the terrain and look for the trail markers, you ride by those flags," she explains. "At times, there is this horrible desire to have it end ASAP."

That's what it can be on good saddles and on your own well-behaved horses. But what was it like to ride in Mongolia on barely-trained little beasts using questionable tack, not even knowing where you were going to sleep that night or how deep the rivers were going to be?

Carol describes it as "loneliness and drudgery on the long days, interspersed with awareness of the beauty of the surroundings and the generosity of the Mongolian people."

I look for other clues to why she does what she does: In high school and college (where she majored in physics), she was a cross-country runner. Her reading interest is polar exploration, she says, books on "trying and freezing to death or drowning, the boat trapped in ice, but I don't have the urge to do that or Everest." I surmise that for Carol, the craving for outdoor action, well-modulated speed, an element of physical danger, autonomy and covering distance seems bred in the bone.

These qualities among others attract increasing numbers of women to endurance riding. According to the AERC records, since 2001 when the membership was sixty-nine percent male, females have taken to the saddle for long distance like crazy: they now constitute eighty-two percent of the membership. And they do well: Of the winners through 2020, thirty-two have been male and thirty-three female.

"Women outride the men in this sport, and men claim it's because we're lightweight," said Juliette Suhr of Scott's Valley, California. Julie is the godmother of endurance racing, having completed twenty-two Tevis Cups out of twenty-nine starts.

I heard and read about her for decades before I called her up to ask how and why she does what she so artfully and successfully does.

"I won—well, my horse HCC Gazal won it three times: he was age seven, eight and ten," she says. Like Carol, she never quits. She completed the Tevis at the age of 76, and attempted it again four years later, coming within two miles of another record finish.

"I think women have more empathy with horses than men, maybe that goes back to nurturing," she tells me. "Women are not as competitive and know when to back off on a horse when it's not going well. That's the secret on hundred-mile rides: When he shows signs of tiring, you have to let him get wind and come back. If he's an honest horse, if you have a good relationship with him, you can read him and decide when he needs encouragement, read signs of fatigue, also learn the individual strengths and weaknesses of horses."

"Ride out and have fun with a horse and the adrenalin flows," Julie said. "When you cross the finish line, you're ten feet tall."

I don't care about racing for days or even hours to a finish line, but I am keen to try both of Carol's horses. So the next day, after a light breakfast, Carol and I depart for a mid-morning ride. It is Saturday, and since the stable is part of a public park, it is open to the public. Non-riders and families wander the barn aisles, pushing kids in strollers, oohing, aahing and doing stupid things around the very indulgent horses.

This time I mount up on Bakari, who instantly feels firm and eager beneath me with more palpable energy than Stetson. As we trot the trail, she flattens her ears, bursts past the gelding, then slows to reconsider and decides she doesn't really want to be in the lead. Flatten, burst, pause. She surges forward, drops back. I cannot stop her or slow her much, so it's a matter of just staying on and trying to keep my knees away from tree trunks.

"I loved horses almost from the very beginning, much to my parents' bafflement (they are completely non-horsey)," Carol tells me. "There was no formative event. Just suddenly everything (toys, books, play, travel destinations) had to be horse-related! I rode my first 'horse' at a very young age (two or three)—one of those plastic palominos suspended from four springs on a stand in our living room."

Now that Carol has done the toughest horserace in the world, what is left to conquer?

"Brian and I would like to do a horse-packing trip in the wilderness, just ourselves, our horses and a pack horse," she tells me. "It's maybe more his dream than mine, because horse-packing would be only walking. There was a couple who rode from South America to Canada—just shoot me now!"

Oh really? And what about the Mongol Derby? Over the course of the Mongol Derby Carol was bucked off twice, and some of her tack fell off.

"It was kind of a rodeo," she says. "The horses are not used to saddles and attached stuff.

"I felt a little under-prepared for Mongolia," she confessed, as we walked briefly in some welcome dappled shade, even though she had been coached for three days by Schork prior to the Derby. "I felt I should be running more, but I have a back issue, so I swam and rode my bike. I was cardiovascularly fit but unprepared for the terrain and getting off the horse and trying to run over rocks and hummocky vines and roots, falling over, running down mountains. Holding the GPS in one hand meant a twist and that led to back spasm—it was tight toward the end of the race."

Four riders from her Derby didn't complete her race. They were hoisted out by the medic team that follows the riders in two vehicles.

"You push the HELP button on your spot tracker, and they get your message, hopefully, and come find you. They take you to the hospital like my friend Matthew and a number of others who got sick in the middle."

There are now so many applicants that Mongol Derby rules allow only first-time entrants—about forty-five at the last one. That number is based on the supply of horses.

"You can cram into the *gers* (Mongolian huts) to sleep—that's no problem," she tells me. "But they need to provide twenty-nine horses per person plus extras because they go lame, get sick or run off."

Gender is no obstacle in this tough and testing race, nor is age. The 2019 Derby was won by a 70-year-old cowboy from Idaho. He, too, emphasized preparation, and, like Carol, as a seasoned endurance rider, he'd had a lifetime of it. Also like her, he mostly rode alone.

Carol approached this epic event with savvy, not macho.

"If I was really stiff in the morning, I'd have a herder ride the horse a bit first," she said. "The horses were like little rockets, but eventually it was just a horse under you, one side for each leg. I rode alone a lot."

"When you are with a horse, you are in the moment, you focus on the horse and what it does, what it needs," Carol tells me. "It quiets your mind when you are in the flow. You are not thinking about the rest of life and your problems."

Exactly, I thought. And for most of us, it doesn't take a hundred taxing, trotting miles or 600-plus galloping miles to feel that amalgam of bliss and relief. Maybe the distance is in proportion to our individual need for quiet and simplicity. Then I was astonished to hear her say, "Now I am at a point where I like being with horses. I don't feel like I need to ride them."

And yet, she later told me: "It doesn't have to be the Derby. I like challenges and feeling I accomplish something. You really get away from the world when you are out there, alone with a horse, no phone, on your own away from civilization."

In the interim, she has to be content with shorter and presumably tamer races. Temptations do still emerge for her, however.

She tells me, "I am headed to South Africa for a 350-kilometer race in October."

She says this without a hint of boasting, not even a flicker of excitement in her voice. It doesn't seem like an addict upping the dosage, just another way to get at the "bliss and relief" perhaps.

Her choice of challenge is Race the Wild Coast, which takes place in a location so remote that riders who quit have to be helicoptered out or suffer a seven-hour bumpy car ride.

"In this one, you have three horses, so you have to manage them," Carol said. "It involves swimming through rivers and some rock slopes like cliffs that you have to scramble down on your own feet."

"It's more technically challenging than the Mongol Derby."

And that derby?

"I want to do it again," she says, as we trot back toward the stable.

"Why?" (For God's sake! I think.)

"I think I can do it better. Faster."*

After riding with Carol, I have absolutely no doubt. Yes, she can.

***Note:** Yes, she did. In 2022, Carol returned to Mongolia to compete in a field of 46 riders. Eight days and 623 miles later, she crossed the Mongol Derby finish line to tie for eleventh place. She keeps going, and between 2008 and mid-2024, she has ridden 3,595 total miles in AERC competitions including several No Frills (formerly Cavalry) but not including the Mongol Derby.

CHAPTER 18

Sightings

"Whatever the pony did was fine by her, because he was her very own pony, and if you were a certain kind of little girl, a pony of your very own was the world's finest treasure, and no matter how many times over the years your mother said, 'It was that awful pony that started all this. I mean, he wasn't even very pretty or nice! I told your father—,' he still remained in your mind as the ultimate good thing."

~Jane Smiley, *Horse Heaven*

At a local YWCA dance class, nine small girls, three- to five-year-olds in tights and leotards, hop, writhe, and leap across the floor. Parents and friends sit along one wall as the teacher, tapping a drum, instructs the kids to pretend to be seals, to make small and large motions, to feel their muscles move. Then, as Enya purls out of the tape player, they obligingly curl up on the floor for a quick "dream."

After two or three silent minutes, the instructor asks the girls "What did you dream?"

"A magic pony..." "a unicorn that would take me anywhere..." "a horse with wings that took me in a tunnel under the sea!" the little voices chorus.

I could rest my case here, but it continues almost daily. I keep casual track of the ways horsegirls crop up in my life. When one pays attention, horsegirls are ubiquitous and not necessarily just in their native habitat, stables, farms and shows.

In a women's clothing store, as the clerk wraps up a necklace for me, I compliment her on her earrings, a pair of silver leaping horses.

"Yes, I love Native American art," she says with a broad smile. "And horses—that's for power!"

At a drugstore, I sift through birthday cards for a friend. Under "Girls' Birthdays" are four card choices: a Barbie-like figure in a pink ball gown; a kitten; flowers; a vaguely Arabian white horse, its mane and bridle decked with tiny pink bows. No horses cavort across cards labeled "Boys' Birthday."

In the women's restroom at the Charlottesville, Virginia, airport, I am washing my hands and scrutinizing a ponytailed young woman at the sink next to me: No makeup, slim, bellbottom jeans and square-toed scuffed brown boots.

"What kind of horses do you have?" I ask, knowing the answer is probably Quarter Horses.

"Is it so easy to tell?" she retorts with a smile.

"Oh yes, it really is," I say.

Her answer is "Quarter Horses."

I would like to know more, but we are both rushed, so I watch her move off down the terminal hallway walking straight, self-possessed, with a certain radiant physicality. This one rides fast, I also know.

Even if I don't encounter one firsthand, I note the secondary effects of having a horsegirl in the family. In a coffee shop one Sunday morning, I spot a middle-aged woman with short black hair wearing a polar fleece horse print jacket with silver buttons.

"Are you a horse lover?" I ask.

No, but she and her husband just dropped their 11-year-old daughter at a barn where she cleans fifty-two stalls in exchange for keeping her own Quarter Horse there.

Flying home to Minnesota from a trip to New York, I am seated next to an older man, who tells me he is the editor of an African American newspaper. His best work, he says, is with homeless inner city kids, and he raises funds to get them to a summer camp in northern Minnesota each year. He chaperones them there, he tells me, and he finds the situation "pretty hopeless," citing pregnancy, dropping out of school, drugs and crime.

"But one thing works, just one thing," he adds.

“What’s that?” I ask. I can guess.

“Horses,” he says. “They really respond to horses. They love to pet them, they learn to take care of something outside themselves, it gives them goals. They all go home talking about the horses.”

At the plant nursery, I strike up a conversation with a woman over her sleek black French bulldog. Out of nowhere she says “We are thinking of getting a miniature horse, too, for my daughter who is five and wants a pony.”

Horse lovers are often recognizable perhaps in the way gay people recognize each other through little subliminal clues. We are not all visibly outdoorsy, not always weathered, tan and lined, especially when young, and not exactly boyish. Horsegirlness is an amalgam of hints in dress, movement, hair and something in the way we carry ourselves, with an energy or perhaps an aura all its own.

Nancy Schapiro trains dogs for Helping Paws, a service that provides dogs to the disabled. She owns a Thoroughbred–Warmblood cross mare named Tir Na. Over lunch she explained to me that Tir Na is Gaelic, a place where Irish faeries dwell, the land of eternal youth.

“I’m hoping she will give me that—eternal youth,” said Nancy, who boards Tir Na at a dressage stable and rides twice a week. “I have such a good time when I ride her. I go to such a childlike state.”

Once more I note that I am encountering and riding with old girls, girls in the guise of women. And horseloving women are so very likely to be dog and cat lovers as well that I expect it.

Nancy tells me her mother died when she was eighteen, and prior to that they fought a great deal, most often about Catholicism. She is married but has no children. “I choose not to, it’s a thankless job,” she says. Her work and play with animals, however, nurtures her at all times and uncountable ways.

“I get so much back from animals that I can’t do enough for them,” Nancy tells me. “Dogs help open my heart in a way people can’t. They are the only ones I let go to a place where I grieve deaths and loss.”

One catch in this investigative expedition is that I am looking for personal truths and the secrets of female emotional lives among women, some of whom may be (by nature and/or as a consequence of their families) more secretive and protective, shy or wounded than others. Horses are the password, however, and if I wait, the women who love them, own them, or desire to own them, will talk with me about the deepest feelings they have.

Whatever it is, whatever we are, it begins early.

On a trip to northern Virginia horse country, I took a riding lesson from former United States Equestrian Team member Phyllis Dawson, a three-day event trainer, at her farm outside Purcellville.

"My first word was 'horsie,'" said Dawson. " I noticed horses no bigger than dots on the horizon when I was just two."

Down the road in Leesburg at the University of Virginia's Equine Medical Center, Carol Miller remembers wanting horses "as far back as I can go—maybe four years old. I remember Dad took me on a pony ride. Even before that I'd watch for the milk wagon horse or a man who would lead two horses down our street to the farrier."

We seek out barns, and we are lucky if we live where no parental transport system is needed to get us there. I could bike or walk to my childhood barn, and I did so daily after school, all day on weekends. Today when I hear someone say "Hey, shut the door! Were you raised in a barn?" I think well, yes, largely.

I can remember more about the barn than about my bedroom, although I recall the four lengths of silky nylon string I tied to the back of my desk chair to teach myself the use of four reins. I put the instruction book on the chair seat and knelt on the rug, looping the snaffle rein (the top string) under my little fingers and the curb rein under the ring fingers. Never mind I was at the time only riding a fiercely indifferent Welsh-Shetland pony with nothing more than baling twine over her lower jaw or a simple Western bridle from the local farm supply store. Thinking about it now, I realize I had dreams I didn't know I had.

Peterson's barn is still in my dreams: a big red dairy barn converted to box and tie stalls, it was set on a hill amid cottonwoods, oaks and ash trees. Whether coated in frost, ice, snowdrifts or sunlight, it was chock full of girls and of ponies and horses of all colors and qualities as well as cobwebs, battalions of mice, treacherous holes in the haymow floor, pitchforks and rusty barbed wire. Someone—sometimes me—was always getting kicked, bitten or tossed off in the road or the cornfield or the sandpit by a runaway. There were great shrieking battles as the barn cats chased rats through the rafters over our heads.

What I saw there, what I was there, was one of the girls who live for horses: often bold, sometimes awkward with people, or considered too loud or too masculine. We doted on critters, from earthworms and caterpillars to Shetlands and draft horses. We spat off the side of our horses, peed in the field, climbed trees, ripped leeches off our toes without getting queasy.

We had something powerful and free-running, and it loved us back.

Then as now, we are rarely indecisive, the result of years of having to make choices at high speed, deciding to rein hard to avoid a hole while galloping over a field. We do not suffer fools, at least not forever, the consequence of being with an animal that cannot lie.

Living a fantasy keeps us Amazons at the core. Not a bad thing in a world that still attempts to squash women into Stepford wives or Sports Illustrated cover girls and discards those who won't or can't fit a mold.

I theorized on this for years, and then went to other members of our tribe to see what they might add.

Pamela Woolley, former director of development for the Marion duPont Scott Equine Medical Center on the edge of Leesburg, Virginia, began riding at seven. She was temporarily steered away to skiing by her family but returned to riding at twenty-two. When not raising funds or marketing the center, she rides her Thoroughbred gelding Grand Tour, affectionately nicknamed Dobbin, in amateur level jumping competitions.

"Horsewomen do seem to have some characteristics in common," she said as we talked one autumn afternoon in her office just off the surgery rooms. With her large direct eyes, bright, short blond hair and a sense of being in a fast idle, she had the intense physical energy I was accustomed to seeing in horsewomen no matter their age.

"It's a lifestyle, not a sport," Pamela pointed out. "It is something that infuses a life."

Then she ticked off a list of qualities that describe most horsewomen, including the two of us.

"The women who do it are adventurous, they push themselves to do things others might not do. Some are staid and controlled and quiet—those tend to be in dressage, but those like me do some other higher-risk horse activities."

Check and check again. I have always been in the second category.

"They are competitive, committed to fitness and health," she continued. "They want a partnership where they don't have to do all the work. They have an appreciation for nature and the outdoors, an aptitude for solitude and quiet. They are people who have a lot of energy and an active life, and they put a lot of effort into finding balance. For me, it's a trick to have time for piano, my friends, family and my horse."

She has paid keen attention, I marveled. And yes, that is me, that is us. And she continued, hitting each mark I had observed as well.

"They are independent," said Pamela, who married at thirty-two and is child-free by choice. "Kids seem like a drag, I'm so busy!" she told me.

"They enjoy the partnership with an animal; it's a physical partnership that builds communication and trust. They have more than the usual creativity, not necessarily in the traditional way in expressing themselves through painting, writing or music but as problem solvers and fixers."

It was thrilling to hear this list, and I couldn't disagree with any of it. Pamela, after all, was in the thick of horse country and had amassed an extensive body of field experience both at the clinic and in her own riding.

"They are exceptionally inquisitive," she continued. "They are learners who collect information and want more data about horses. They are trendy but not trendsetters in terms of studying training methods. And they want to have fun!"

"There's a subset who are more spiritual, more romantic about the horse relationship," she concluded. "They see a horse as something to caretake, they fuss and worry about it."

That would be many women I know as well, including those who don't care to ride much if at all.

Many of these characteristics are found in women who do other sports. With the right mix of nerve, energy, outdoorsiness and independence, etc., why not turn to rock climbing, sailing, skiing or whitewater canoeing? That's the distinction I was after.

The components those sports lack (and they are sports, not the all-consuming phenomenon of horses) is relationship to an animal—the opportunity for communication, nurturing, adventure and partnership.

It's what I see in the daydreams of little girls, in the desires and schemes of teens, in the ardor of females of all ages. It is a distinct, deep-seated compulsion, despite injuries, danger and not-infrequent fear.

It is evident in my goddaughter Allie taking cross-country timber fences in three-day events on her Warmblood mare. It is evident when Briana, a teen girl barrel racer, blasts around the barrels in all-out galloping turns aboard Junior, her grandfather's Quarter Horse. It is evident when my friend Sharon hitches her plump black Morgan mare to a cart and trots down the gravel backroads.

It is evident that there is an almost palpable feedback loop, a torrent of unique feeling, that returns to a girl with her pony, a woman with her horse.

CHAPTER 19

Wild at Heart

> ***"You're a fourteen-year-old girl . . . You all have a thing for horses and wolves. I love that. I love that. That's so weird. What is that about?"***
>
> **~Emily Fridlund, *History of Wolves***

Belle, her name was Belle. I thought it was Bell, being only eight or nine and not yet introduced to the poetry of French as applied to women or horses.

I met her because my Dad knew a guy. Dad always knew a guy who (fill in the blank): tumbled rocks, made knives, tanned deer hides, brewed beer, grew capons, had a trout farm, smoked carp in his backyard, collected antique cars, etc.

This particular guy, Dad's friend Mel-in-the-insurance-business, owned a farm on the edge of town just past the vegetable market, where one day Mel, Dad, and I and several of Mel's scrambly kids walked out through the summer grass. Mel whistled toward the old oaks and cottonwoods.

A red-gold creature came ripping and rolling and snorting up the meadow, her long head held high on a neck like a sea serpent. Her large hooves flew upward and paddled outward, a full udder of milk heaved side to side under her flank as she galloped toward the coffee can of oats he shook.

Her colt followed her, ping-ponging along like a baby giraffe, fuzz-tailed and spring-legged.

Belle was the most feminine, moist, dark-eyed, warm-skinned exotic thing

I'd seen, smelling of milk and grass, breathing like a steam engine.

Years later, I know she was an American Saddlebred. At the time, I thought she was Pegasus' mother—especially when I was hoisted up on her bare back.

Dad led us around the field, and I felt clouds below me, above me, around me.

Grownups fell away. Time fell away. There was a hush.

I saw what I needed, wanted, was. This was power and majesty, adventure, escape and things beyond my ability to describe them then and possibly even now.

Decades later, I see that look, that electrification, the first time I put a child or an adult onto a horse or pony bareback. There is that same hush. Their eyes widen, they look out and away over the mane of the horse. They look down at me. We both know something ineffably wondrous is happening.

Some visitors (almost all of them male) to my pasture take a look and refuse to get on my horse. Otherwise, this very thing that gripped me aboard Belle that childhood summer day happens to everyone willing to try it.

After I boosted one young man onto my chestnut Thoroughbred, he sat silently a few minutes. Then he said, "This is more than a sport, isn't it?" Exactly so, sir.

I sat on Belle that summer day, and for the next decade or so I sought horses and noted horse images from the Pegasus signs over the local gas station (red, white and winged—no company would have such a romantic logo now) to the Kentucky Club Tobacco in fragrant blue and black tins. That company held a "name the Thoroughbred colt and win it" contest: I sent in thirty names and prayed.

I didn't yet own one, but horses were my landmarks, my aspiration, inspiration and dream. I got greedy about it, too.

At the annual county fair, my middle sister Gayle and I fought over the ponies trudging around chained in the pony ride ring: "Mine!" "No, that one's mine, the pinto and that one." "Okay, but then I get this black one and that one with the blue eyes."

At Fourth of July parades, our bottoms on the curb and sneakers in the gutter, Gayle, our youngest sister Jill and I watched local beauties perched on crepe-festooned floats and high school marching bands sweltering in wool uniforms. I waited most of all for the clatter of the Sunset Saddle Club, the local riders that traditionally brought up the rear of the parade.

Sisters were useful: We could make a case that Molly the pony was not enough for three. With Sugar and her colt, Gabe, we amassed a small herd. Dad paid $30 a summer for a pasture to a Norwegian immigrant, a postman named Peder Olsen and his daughter Palma. In winter, at Peterson's barn atop the hill next to the pasture, the cost was $2.50 a month for a tie stall, $5 a month for a box stall. The dads paid, dads who were furniture store owners, auctioneers, electricians, plumbers, and our dad, the chiropractor.

For those of us who lived in town, our parents took us girls to shows, rising at 5 a.m. on summer weekends to get the horses primped. I applied coconut shampoo that made Gabe smell edible, then scrubbed stains out of his white mane and tail. I wrapped his damp tail in an athletic bandage from Dad's office and covered him with old bed blankets to keep him clean until competition time: halter class, Western pleasure, equitation, egg and spoon, barrel races, pickup races with my friend Polly aboard her speedy gray mare Lady.

And for me, for a summer or two, there were wolves, also because Dad knew a guy. Unlike horses, wolves were something I rarely saw but also loved. I dearly wanted them to exist in what little ground was left to them by trophy hunters and the rancher/farmer "shoot, shovel, and shut up" crowd.

I had grown up steeped in Rudyard Kipling, especially *The Jungle Book* and loved the idea of being raised by wolves. They seemed then and even more now, to be true higher animals. Besides, it was Kipling who had written "Four things greater than all things are—Women and Horses, and Power and War." A wolf pack was not going to take me in, and Kipling was not around for me to ask him the rationale behind his esteem for women and horses. So I made do.

The guy Dad knew lived in what was then considered a radically modern style cedar-shingled house set off the slope of the county highway. Tucked on the flat below the house was a small barn, a kennel and a chain link dog run with a shed attached. The guy had Arabian horses "that needed riding," I was told. I obliged him during one or two summers when I was home from college.

No one said I could and no one said I couldn't go into that kennel run. And no one was supervising. So I did.

Her name was Susie, and I don't recall whether she was half timber wolf or all wolf. She was, like wolves I came to know much later, thoroughly quiet and very shy. I mostly just sat with her in her run, side by side, being still together. We watched the horses, curvy, small bay Arabians. She was never, to my knowledge, let out of that concrete and chain link cage.

Years later, as a reporter working on a story on wolf issues, I joined wildlife biologist and wolf expert Dr. David Mech in the northern Minnesota woods.

We stood in the dark among the pines and howled, our noses to the sky, and listened for a reply.

About that time, wolves were being reintroduced to Yellowstone National Park, and subsequently a *Star Tribune Sunday Magazine* staff photographer and I stopped at the Jackson, Wyoming, headquarters of The Wolf Project to interview the director. We searched for days but saw no wolves, just their primordial landscape.

Years after that, I was in a dew-spangled sleeping bag atop a hill on the Thorstein Veblen family plot in a small Norwegian immigrant cemetery in Minnesota. Well on toward dawn, first one voice tuned up, then two, then more, and the oaks below the hill echoed with the yips and quavers of a pack.

"Thank you," I whispered to the October night sky. I didn't know until a day later that a family just over the hill kept a few Mackenzie Valley wolves on their farm.

Further years on, working in a large Midwest humane society, I sat alone on a dog crate in the loading dock while two dozen wolves paced their cages in silence around me. They walked back and forth for hours, not so much distressed perhaps as perplexed. A woman who had kept them chained in the desolate Wisconsin backwoods had died, and someone was alert enough and kind enough to call my humane society. We placed them with a Western-state sanctuary.

The wolf and the horse: Do they intertwine in the subconscious? Do they devolve in our racial memory? Are freedom and the joy of wild hearts what they share and symbolize to us?

I know they attract, console and inspire me and myriad others. And the one that agrees to be owned in return is the horse.

CHAPTER 20

Horses on the Brain

"You could take all my material possessions away from me, and I'd get along, but I would have to have one horse to look at out the window. It's such a comforting sight. It's sort of an obsession isn't it?"

~Juliette Suhr, *Endurance riding champion*

My brain is sticky for animals, horses in particular. Dogs and cats come in a close—and quite different—second.

I am walking around a local lake taking part in an informal Midwestern version of the *paseo* (promenade), except here nobody flirts as in Spain, where the evening parade around the city fountain is an excuse to size each other up.

Round we go in pairs or singles or fours, walking our corgipoos, dachsipoos, berniepoos, chuwienies (Chihuahua crossed with Dachshund). Although I have never before seen one in real life, I recognize a Chinese Chin trotting along the path. I spot a Wirehaired Pointing Griffon (a bird dog) and then a hound I've seen only in books, something Italian. I look it up quickly: it's a Bracco Italiano.

What determines our affinities?

No, that is not a strong enough term.

What determines our passions, obsessions, addictions? Why am I kissing, petting and talking to dogs (and have done so from when I could crawl under the table and grab our Dachshund), while other people are intensely attracted to bowling, softball, NASCAR or knitting? What neural pathways exist for those of us countless females who respond to animals and in particular equines?

A sleep expert I heard on the radio described something as a "deep hedonic reward"—perhaps just an academic way of saying pleasure. I think what we experience in the presence of horses, at least some of us, is more. Chocolate causes a pleasure response. What I am tracking, what I experience, is more widespread than pleasure, more acute than simple sweetness and deeper than delight.

And although those who believe we are more nurture than nature will disagree, I also have come to believe it is a genetic propensity, even an edict.

So now I am seeking someone who can unpack the neurology of attraction/addiction, of a more-than-pleasure response.

To paraphrase an unforgettable ad: This is your brain. This is your brain on horses. Or, for that matter, any equine.

For example, I am supposed to be listening to my yoga instructor, but I am thinking about mules: Five roly-poly blond mules in the pasture across the gravel road from my horses. Their big dark eyes under heavy brows, their tranquil welcoming faces and soft, seeking lips, their joy when one runs and they all join in stiff-legged, bouncing on their small round hooves, farting and aiming faux kicks at each other.

This leads me to thinking about another donkey, a 15.3-hand mammoth jenny (mare), a dark bay with a cream belly. Her fringed ears stand out like mighty stalks from her head. Her name is Alora, and she has been owned since birth by my friend Tabea. When Tabea calls to her from thousands of yards away, out of sight across the barnyard, she gives a thin answering whistle, wavery and keen, not a hee haw, but fine and intense.

"I would give my life for her," Tabea tells me. I suspect the feeling is mutual.

For those of us obsessed, even if we don't own them or ride them, they are even satisfying to simply watch—what is that?

Carrots and sticks? Horses are my carrots: if I promise to sit at the computer for x hours, then I will allow myself the carrot of an afternoon, or better, a morning, to ride.

This is, of course, backwards from the leading-a-horse-with-a-carrot thing, which works pretty well, although it tends to result in bad manners on the part of the horse.

What does a psychological icon have to say about this phenomenon, our horse love?

I forge into a bit of Carl Jung writing about his interpretation of the dream experience of a 17-year-old girl. It leads him to this: "Horse is an archetype that is widely current in mythology and folklore. As an animal it represents the non-human psyche, the subhuman, animal side, the unconscious. That is why horses in folklore sometimes see visions, hear voices, and speak. As a beast of burden it is closely related to the mother-archetype (witness the Valkyries that bear the dead to Valhalla, the Trojan horse, etc.). As an animal lower than man, it represents the lower part of the body and the animal impulses that rise from there. The horse is dynamic and vehicular power: it carries one away like a surge of instinct. It is subject to panics like all instinctive creatures who lack higher consciousness. Also it has to do with sorcery and magical spells—especially the black night-horses which herald death."

In grade school, some kids called me Whinny-ger. I didn't mind much, because even at six and seven, it was evident that I *was* horse crazy. Model horses and horse books were not going to satisfy my craving to ride beyond the merry-go-round at the county fair, to be with real horses. Within two or three years of constant wheedling, begging and writing letters to Santa, I was given that pony. Molly never then or now seems to represent death, the unconscious or a mother, but she was absolute magic for me.

Girls in more urban populations now show the same desire, but how is it satisfied? Is it satisfied? Who exploits that desire?

Prowling through YouTube, I glimpse a road show musical born of the My Little Pony toy. It is all bulbous foreheads and long-lashed eyes, wings, unicorn horns and rainbow tails—and that was all on a single actor. The marketing was as overblown as the costuming: "dazzling all-new stage musical ready to entertain and delight! Featuring an original story, follow Twilight Sparkle, Pinkie Pie, Rarity, Fluttershy, Applejack, and Rainbow Dash (with Spike in tow!) as the beloved ponies embrace their true colors and embark on a magical adventure. Come one pony, come all, on this unforgettable journey to Equestria! Don't miss *My Little Pony Live*, the ultimate celebration of laughter, kindness, and the magic of friendship."

These were not horses to me in any sense, and I doubt they would have been satisfactory to my child self. What I craved then was the real thing in all its dimensions, even when it kicked me, bit me, scraped me into trees, bucked me off or ran away with me. What I crave now are also answers and amplification on my theories.

Jung had mentioned horses as connected to dynamic power, the lower body, sorcery and magic and, of course, instinct. It's nice to have academic, scientific validation for a hunch or at least corroboration for my sense of horse love. Dr. Anne Perkins gave me a more current confirmation.

Perkins was not twenty-four hours back from a fifty-mile ride on her senior Arabian when I pounced on her in Helena, Montana. She was heading to the barn to work with her three-year-old (horse, not child). Later she would prepare for a conference at the University of Montana in Dillon where her topic is the genetics of the human–animal bond.

"Horses and women are completely intertwined," she asserted. "I see this playing out in everything I hold true from scholarly experiences."

Perkins holds a doctoral degree in animal behavior and created the Human-Animal Bond Program, now Anthrozoology, at Carroll College, a small institution in Helena, Montana. The classes encompass both dog and horse connections with people. They are so popular that the program swiftly evolved from a minor in 2006 to a major in 2011. And guess who is enrolling?

"Anthrozoology demographics are like those of most all equine sports: about 97 percent of these students are women," Perkins said. "This is way beyond statistically significant."

Like me, like so many of us, she grew up on a literary diet that included Marguerite Henry's books. As a teen, she took lessons in exchange for work at a local stable. At fifteen, she won her first horse in an essay contest; the subject was how you would take care of a horse if you had one.

Could all this somehow be genetic, I asked her.

"From a co-evolutionary perspective, when zoologists and biologists talk about co-evolution, mutualism means both species benefit," said Perkins. "When we talk about domestication, however, we talk about how humans change animals, we never talk about how animals change humans. I believe we who love horses like we do are survivors: our ancestors were very successful at working with horses, that's why they survived. That relationship gave them an advantage over some people who were not."

So yes, we inherit this aptitude, this passion. Millennia ago, horse love gave us an edge in some ways as did love of dogs.

The reinforcement that humans get from animal companions is unique, says Perkins. At Carroll College, where she developed both canine and equine programs, "colleagues told me to just do the dogs. It's much easier, the insurance is less, and you don't need a barn. I said, 'We have to do the horse program. It is different. I want graduates to experience that horse experience and vice versa.'"

"In my classes, I've witnessed students with the least amount of horse experience are most impacted by the opportunity to interact with horses," she continued. "They hang out at the barn, do work study and are deeply grateful for the chance to get to know horses on an intimate basis. Some just stand next to a horse and start crying."

This intimacy can vary by individual and tends to vary by gender. She notes this takes place both in the academic setting and in the world at large.

"Men appreciate and enjoy their horses, too," Perkins said. "I think for most men it's about a tool or a service the horse provides. For women, it's more about the relationship. I literally love my horses. I have authority over and responsibility for them, and we are partners in getting through the task. They are not my tools, and they are not surrogates for children."

Before she retired him, Perkins and her Arabian gelding, Jamel, were an endurance team, and they completed requirements for an AERA Decade Team Award: one 50-mile ride in each of ten years, including 50 miles along the Continental Divide in Montana.

"When a guy goes on a pack trip on a horse to go hunting or fishing, or when he rounds up cows or wins money at an event, it's a competition," she observes. "It's about their horse is better than yours. For women, a horse is a sanctuary to get away from the stress of the world, to be with an animal that is picky about who they are with. Being with a horse empowers women, and it doesn't matter to the horse if you are not popular or pretty. A horse confirms your value."

"Similar to dogs, horses are part of the family," she adds. "A big difference is horses are a gigantic, powerful prey species. Arabians especially can be anxious and flighty. And it is really hard to get a horse to partner with you as opposed to do what you ask. If they choose to partner with you, it is an overwhelming sense of joy and companionship."

In the college program "we teach some round pen stuff," Perkins explains. "If you do it right, a horse will choose to be with you. When students experience that, it is so affirming and it impacts them in very positive ways. It doesn't feel the same when a dog wags his tail at you, as they will do that for many people. The horse says 'Maybe you are good enough to be my leader' or 'I experience positive energy from you.'"

"I don't think there is a human who can provide another human with that kind of reinforcement," she told me, and I cheered silently at her candor. This can be particularly distinctive with wild horses, said Perkins, who spent three years on a study of wild horses with filmmaker Ginger Kathrens in the Pryor Mountain Wild Horse Range, the same place I had visited.

"Horses live in bands, and nothing is stronger than what those mares in those bands have with each other," she tells me. "If they bond to you like wild mares bond with their mates, you are golden. That is the goal, to embed yourself in their ability to bond that tightly. So when you are riding them, and they want to go back to the barn, they are not barn sour (reluctant to leave the stable). It's that they are not in love with you."

How can we learn Bonding 101? This academically innovative major she has created is what thousands of clinicians, acclaimed trainers and self-proclaimed horse whisperers are reaching for, I thought.

If you are born a horsegirl—and since talking with her, I am closer than ever believing it is genetic—I suspect you might have the instinct to do it right. You can improve on your techniques, but the affinity must be in place at the beginning.

How are their rare, trusting and loving relationships with humans best formed, I asked.

"I *know* what to do, it is inside me, and I feel what I need to do to gain this sacred critter to bond to me," she explained. "Everything I did to befriend a Mustang was exactly intuitive. For example, it doesn't seem right to tie him down. You get on slowly, never, ever buck 'em out. If I want to partner with him on the range, I need him to be safe, go slow, earn his confidence. Once they bond to me and I am their leader, they know 'I won't hurt you, we are a team, we trust each other.' This is in my heart and my genetics, and it is confirmed in my academic experience."

The genetics of the horse are at play as well.

"Some are docile, less anxious and more comfortable being domesticated; others carry high anxiety genes, are more nervous and less likely to bond, but when they do it is big time."

I think of Gabe and Shadow, my two not-too-distantly-related gray Arabians. With them I spent intimate time, massive and life-changing time. And that's why the grief is so deep when they pass.

Perkins is speaking in part of Jamel but also of Mustangs and of her other horses when she says "I have a horse carry me fifty miles, come up to me when I call it, or tell me with its eyes when something is wrong." There's the bond.

Then she says clearly what I have thought for long years, mostly in private, that possibly explains horsegirldom: "So you are responsible for that, and you listen to them in a way that you are genetically engendered to do."

Until we can slide a number of willing horse crazy females into an MRI or scrape their cheeks and twirl the tissue down to the target chromosomes, I will have to accept that this is as much as we can glean, penetrate or describe of this mystery. Our fascination is innate, our calling was cast long ago and is engraved in us. And if we are very, very lucky, we follow it all our lives.

Gone Riding

"Horse crazy. It happens to a lot of little girls. I think my case was fairly modest considering the more virulent strains of this epizootic. When I watched cowboy movies (and God knows I'm still a sucker for a Republic Western), it was the horse that held me in thrall. And while I had guns and holsters aplenty, my interest wasn't in the gunfight at the OK Corral, but riding off into the sunset on Topper, or Champion, or Trigger, Tarzan, Diablo, or Silver."

~ Candyce Barnes,
"Boots, Saddle, to Horse, and Away" in
***Horse People*, an anthology edited by Michael Rosen**

I have two choices: the dark, heavy horse whose force is bound in a body of immense slow power or the light, fast horse who dances and startles at every sight and sound.

The dark gelding's coat is soft as sheared beaver. The color is like the ripe skin of an eggplant mixed with sorghum, deep and rich; his pelt ripples over a round body. The tips of his thick black tail, sunburnt auburn as the sea-bleached ends of a Tahitian dancer's hair, fall in plump spirals from broad haunches and skim the ground.

His mane pours over his right shoulder. Legs like fence posts, a wide fore-head with a white star, massive round jowls give him a sense of weight, contravened by a little accent mark of a wrinkle over each eye that shows me he worries about the furred, toothed things in the shadows, about the school bus rattling up the road. It tells me, too, that he has hopes: Is there an apple in my pocket or not? Will there be a meal soon? Will I spread molasses on his bit this time? Is his gelding best friend coming with us?

The other gelding is a desert horse with a deep, noble pedigree, a brooding, swift prince. He is slim and leggy with a wispy mane and long delicate tail, a coat the color of old ivory, a horse of the dry texture and fineness of bone china. Running free, he skims the ground, covers the entire pasture in seconds, his tail cocked over his back, joyfully stampeding himself with monsters of his own imagining, his breath whooshing through huge nostrils dilated wide to a pink lining.

When I sit on the top fence rail and rub the swell of his shapely forehead, the bulge of intelligence that Bedouins call the *jibbah,* he lowers his small, tense chin across my thighs and closes his eyes, chewing and licking, a unicorn in a medieval tapestry dreaming with its head in the lap of a virgin.

They are my yin and yang of horses, stolid and dark, electric and airy. Nothing I say to some people can convince them that Shadow, the Arabian, is a gelding. People introduced to him insist on calling him "she." Men especially assume my dark Percheron-Morgan, Smokey, is a stallion, although he too is a gelding.

Bareback is best for riding either of them. A saddle insulates from the centaur-sense of heft and heat, the exquisite smallness of skin twitch and the softness of a barrel against my ankles, calves and knees.

I grab a twist of mane and leap from a fence rail, the horse eager and moving on—a show of bad manners, I know—before I land.

To the tempo of his walk, ah-one, ah-two, ah-one, ah-two, I break at the waist like a belly dancer. His ribs sway right and left and right and left. His mane wafts up in a roll, flicking my hands.

If I ride the white horse, his body shortens and tenses lightly beneath me, he chews and champs, his soft mouth feels every pulse of blood through my palms and fingers. His preferred speed is a canter that surges into gallop in a millisecond. I work my hands down low on his shoulders, holding him back. "Easy, easy," I whisper, drawing out the vowels.

Riding a trail along the shore of a small lake, we jump poplar trees felled across our path by beavers. He gathers in a half rear and uncoils high over the tree, far higher than needed, and is gone another ten yards before I can rein him back. Curveting on the tips of his fine hooves, his nostrils crimped like the slits of a camel's nose, he flings his head up with excitement, the crest of his neck nearly striking my face.

If I ride the black horse, we rumble over the stubble of corn fields and down gravel roads and up deep grass trails to the tops of low hills. His preferred tempo is the trot. His thick neck shudders as his short legs move in a softly rhythmic one-two, one-two beat. As his body warms, his hair mats down into fine alluvial fans as if the great wash of a river has passed over his neck, breastbone and shoulders.

I ride myself into peace, into calm and always into joy. If I ask them, either horse will prance or stamp onward, never mind the foam of sweat, thick as shaving cream, that appears on their chests and between their thighs.

One night in a snowless early December, I rode Smokey east along the old gravel road to a state park, timing the ride to catch the full moon rising over the river valley.

My hands told him one thing—stay on the usual trail—but I pictured another direction, off the path and straight through the uncut grasses of an old farm field. He heard that deeper wish and struggled against the bit until I gave in, and we did what we both really wanted. Color drained away in the dimming light, but I could still pick out bittersweet, a looping tangle of cinnabar berries gleaming against yew, oak and cedar.

The fields were dry, soundless as if something great held its breath. We traversed a shallow scoop of a mudhole dark and punctuated by deer tracks. A moon shadow of a horse followed us, flowed alongside in the sharpening light of the rising moon.

On a wide meadow sloping down to the river, I reined him to a halt, and we listened. A high descending squeal pierced the gully below old yews, answered by a short chorus of squeals—foxes? coyote pups?—in reply.

Deer stirred in the dark. The black horse heard and fidgeted. I felt them, too, tracking them not by moving air or sound, but by a more ancient way of listening, a thrumming tension in the jawbones, the scalp, ears and skin of my face drawn tight by the rise of tiny hairs.

Pulled by the moon, the warmth, the promise of pine pollen or fireflies or the first frog song when the snow still lingers under the pines, I have ridden this way, most often alone, for decades. We ride and halt, listening in a field above the muskrat lodges, scouting the sky for great blue herons soaring south on the spring wind, their melodic screeches like pterodactyls. We ride and thrill to deer in the dusk, reduced to white throats and tails and something darker between. Ride and watch as a half-dozen wild turkeys heave out of the pines and flap darkly over our heads, weighty as World War II bombers.

Like weapons for battle or flies for fly-fishing, I choose my horse for each ride. The weather, the terrain, the possibility of unwanted traffic in the form of dogs, motorcycles and school buses, how much I feel like going straight or dancing sideways. Whether I want to focus on legs, hands and voice or just dream along atop a warm back determine which one I ride.

Shadow, so light in his bones, bright of mind and imagination, is so perpetually terror-stricken that I nicknamed him Afraid of His Own. He seems comforted when we ride with our built-in game beater, a chocolate Doberman cross named Summer. The dog lopes ahead, tags jingling, flushing wild turkey and pheasant, deer, barred and great horned owls, and the occasional fox, skunk or woodchuck. Her bark descends into whimpering, then into huffing as she runs—always too slowly—after deer.

On Shadow, I shorten reins and grab a hank of mane before we canter up rises, tackle tight turns and over jumps, the better to hold my bareback seat at speed and through occasional lightning lateral swerves.

Smokey is my woolly mammoth, my oak table of a horse, my dark charger. His mind is less lively, his fear thicker and slower. Standing with immense quiet alone in the pasture, he dreams and watches far horizons, lonely for his huge colthood herd or watching for wolves, I imagine.

Best of all is to take them both with me, riding one horse, allowing the other to run alongside or behind, the free horse snatching mouthfuls of grass and nipping at the flanks of the ridden horse, bucking and farting for joy as we canter trails and across fields. Summer filters through the grass with us, dashing occasionally into the lake, spooking the geese, shaking water from her coat and catching up again. Our little herd of horses, dog, horsewoman.

I take few women and fewer men riding. Among my girlfriends are some who are afraid of horses, who confuse size with ferocity, because once as a child they were bucked off (which usually means they fell off) or run away with (which usually means they were assigned the wrong horse and given no operating instructions) or scraped off, which likely means they were too young, timid or inexperienced to guide the horse's action.

"Horses are basically just big rabbits," I tell them, "or big deer." After saying this for years, I was delighted to discover that poet Joy Harjo of the Creek tribe says the Creek word for horse, *rokko*, means big deer.

I try to convey how it's quite natural for a 130-pound woman to boss around a 1,200-pound horse. I tell them that horses inhabit big bodies, but they don't know their power. The trick is not to let them find that out.

"Riding" is shorthand for all that precedes and follows. Riding is not just being astride a horse but also the rituals before and after.

In a barn, I sweep the aisles, fork out manure, cup my hands in the mound of feed, sniff and savor salt and molasses, corn and bran. I take a scrub brush to a water tank dank with glossy green slime. I tote away a winter's worth of empty feed bags crumpled in a corner, hang curry combs, scissors and hoof picks on nails, gather up the baling twine that has drifted around the paddock. To the metronome tick of the electric fence charger, sparrows flutter and skirmish in the rafters, waiting for the golden spatter of oats under my feet.

The list in my head goes away. The list is a jittering ticker tape of needs and duties: the house needs list, the grocery list, the hardware-store-post-office-laundry list, the office duties undone list, the worries about family list, the friends I need to contact list, the birthdays and anniversaries list, the exercise class I keep postponing list.

Around horses, I am absolved. I am doing this in this time and nothing but this.

Around horses, if I do not pay attention this moment and this one and this one, it will mean injury sooner or later. Around horses, distraction can be deadly, for them as well as for me.

I brush tangles and remove burrs. I clean hooves, wielding a small hoof pick shaped like a seven, probing for stones, prying packed manure and dirt out of the crevices around the rubbery triangle whimsically called the frog. The aroma is like a ripe, soft French cheese, at once both repellent and attractive. The meat of the hoof is white and rich, faintly marbled with fine blue-black lines.

When a farrier works, sending chewy flakes of excess hoof like slices of fresh coconut to the barn floor, the farm dogs snatch them up greedily.

And there are other scents: the nut-like scent of his chestnuts, soft pale ovals of horn that are vestigial toes on the inside of his legs. The odor of his sheath, primitive as truffle oil, wafting up from his flanks.

With my nose close to the corner of his mouth, the plump round jowl, his neck, barrel or rump, I move my face along his body, like a cat marking its owner, savoring the sweet, slightly toasted scent as if the heat of his body pumped through each hair had gently singed it. When his coat is damp, the hair over his chest, flanks and shoulders curls into tiny precise curves like the closely packed breast feathers of a pheasant.

I scratch the firm cartilage of his ears, the base of the tail where hair thins out to black skin, and he lifts his tail in pleasure. My hands run over the crest of his neck, pinching as hard as I can, as if they were horse teeth. I tickle his armpit, scratch the bulky elbow where the shoulder meets the barrel. He lowers his head, his upper lip moves back and forth, and if I get the spot exactly right, he clicks his teeth as if he were grooming me in return.

In college, I took courses in Zen Buddhism with a *roshi*, a Buddhist priest, from Kyoto. With two dozen other students, I rose in the dark to walk to the gym and sit silently in meditation—*zazen*—as the sunrise warmed the room. The intent was in part to calm the mind and body by focusing on the breath. I sat dutifully and hopefully on my cushion each morning, cross-legged, hands in lap, eyes closed, back straight. My body fidgeted and ached, my mind yammered on in a little staccato clatter of worry and desire. Sometimes we creaked up off our cushions for *sanzen*, walking meditation, circling silently, our socks scuffing softly on the maple floor.

I don't think of riding as moving meditation, yet here it is, my almost daily devotions, the ritual of grooming and riding, cleaning and contemplation in the presence of horse.

When it works, we are beyond blood and bone of horse thought/human thought, like a shared reel of film running through my chest and deep into his barrel, looping around again.

Riding, I see with horse senses and react with horse-style gasps and snorts and self-soothing: forms scamper atop a hill a quarter mile away, *whuh!* Just dogs, just dogs. Car with lights on, *whuh! whuh!* Hay bales tipped over, *phoooo!* No, just cows, just cows.

At the march tempo of the trot and the swift waltz of the canter, we dance to finger and heel, hips and voice. Not just body driving body, but mind moving mind, I travel with Smokey, Shadow and, weaving through the alders and hazelnuts, the hurrying shape of Summer.

"I cannot remember a time when I didn't love horses," I am told over and over when I ask women when it began for them. It is true for me as well. I suspected that it goes far back, perhaps in racial memory or our DNA. My long years of asking have confirmed it for me.

As horsegirls, part of us never ages, never outgrows that thrum of delight as we watch, smell or touch horses or clear a jump at a hand gallop.

In a wordless understanding, whenever we are with horses, we are most ourselves and something more than ourselves.

They give us awe and comfort, and when we are with them we are now and forever free and young. What could be better?

Acknowledgments

So many people have answered my questions, shared their stories, allowed me to meet their horses, ponies, mules or donkeys. In addition to those mentioned in the preceding chapters, my thanks go to editor Patricia Morris, who is not a horse lover but got it on the first read. Heaps of gratitude go to Joan Nygren of Nygren Design, a heckuva proofreader as well as production manager who always had my back. (And my back needs having.) Author, naval historian and friend William Hammond III provided wisdom from the far side of the world. Writer, scholar and collector Robin Bledsoe, owner of Robin Bledsoe, Bookseller and author, editor and horseman Norm Fine both used their respective vast knowledge of horse literature and horse people to make this a more accurate book. My long time collaborator, photographer Judy Olausen, always makes me look better in black and white than in real life. My cousin Kathy Nielsen provided her discerning eye and regular support. Hugs to Bonnie Harris, friend and marketing whiz, who returned safely to the horse world on the back of my dear Smokey. Blessings on Maciek Gralinski of Technophobia.com because I can harness and drive a team but I can't fathom a computer. Thanks to Jen Weers for her scholarly skills in creating the index and spotting wee errors. Lynn Dosch's steadfast supply of uplifting cards cheered me on over the years it took to complete this. My friend Stacy Schultz, who once served as my Thoroughbred when I dressed as a jockey for the Oakwood School Halloween party, shared her ponderings on our shared passion. To Mary Alexandra McEachern for prodding, smart conversations, fun and a comfortable bed. Thanks to Jen Kelly who introduced me to the writing of Anna Blake. Gratitude to Daniel and Jennifer Lunceford from Maryland, who took a chance on a stranger in a rainstorm and got me to Lexington. A huge dose of gratitude to the Whitaker family of White Bear Lake whose pasture and land were my refuge and retreat for forty-some years. Mike McAllister's loving daily devotion to "our " horses for all those years made my herd possible. My friend Laurie Schneider, a photographer and critter lover, still does most of the work with our beloved Dusty Darcy Darling while I have most of the fun. Speaking of which, my gratitude goes to the late Amy Rubins and her husband Dr. Jeff for the gift of our exquisite rescued horse. My former colleague Sarah T. Williams, a horsegirl herself, did the ferocious and fast final proofing. And bottomless gratitude to the late Peter Vaughan of the late *Minneapolis Star* who did the crucial thing and long ago hired me. And gratitude beyond gratitude and beyond the grave to my grandparents Wallace Aulls Winegar Sr. and Gladys Dietrich Winegar, Harley Greenwalt and Myrtle Linsley Greenwalt. for sending the horsey stuff down the DNA helix to me.

Index

A

Abraham, Susan, 49–51
advocates, for wild horses, 37, 40
AERC (American Endurance Ride Conference), 123–124
aesthetics, horse love and, 96
After Ikkyu and Other Poems (Harrison), 16–17
Allie (goddaughter), 86–87
American Endurance Ride Conference (AERC), 123–124
American Horse Publications (AHP), 89
American Wild Horse Campaign, 40
Amish men, horse conversation with, 3
anatomy, of females vs males for riding, 118
ancestral horse relationships, 144
animal
  -human bond, 144–145 (*see also* bond, females and horses)
  lovers, horsewomen as, 92–93, 133
  psyches of humans and, 99
appreciation, feelings of, 56
Arabian Kill Pen and Auction Horse Group/The Arabian 300 Club (rescue group), 104–105
Arabians (horse breed), 8, 104, 124, 145
auction industry, equine, 102–106, 108–109. *See also* rescue organizations, equine

B

Bagnold, Enid, 10
Ballard, Carroll, 13
Baragli, Paolo, 56
barns. *See* stables/barns
Baskfield, Lynn, 100
beach horse ride, 119
beauty, horse love and, 96
BHSA (British Horse Society Association), 66
"big lick" competitions, 96
binding sweethearts, 16–17. *See also* marriage
Black Beauty (Sewell), 8, 11
Black Stallion, The (Farley), 13
Bledsoe, Robin, 12
BLM (Bureau of Land Management), 38, 40
bodies, of females vs males for riding, 118
bodily freedom, 89
bond, females and horses. *See also* horsegirls/horsewomen
  as genetic (*see* genetic predispositions, of horse love)
  heart horses and, 54–57
  as innate (*see* innate, horse love as)
  reasons for (*see* horse lovers as females, suppositions for)
  relational nature of horses and, 9, 50–51, 75, 95–96, 145
books, equine, 7–13
  by Cumming, 92
  females as main readers of, 9
  horsewomen essence portrayed in, 10–11
  influential to Winegar as child, 8–9, 12–13
  library of, 11–12
  riders as readers, 12
  shelving of at bookstores as prestige-less, 7–8
boys/men. *See* males
British Horse Society Association (BHSA), 66
Brock, Tabea, 32
bronc riding, 67
Brown, Rita Mae, 23
Brune, Chris, 89
Bureau of Land Management (BLM), 38, 40

C

carriage driving, 71–78
  dangers of, 77–78
  females in, 72, 76–77
  gear for, 74–75
  Gloria and (*see* Gloria (carriage driver))
  horses for, 74
  lessons for, 76
  team makeup of, 72–73
  whips and, 73
  by Winegar, 21, 23, 72, 97–98
cattle ranchers, wild horses and, 38, 40
Cavalry category, of endurance riding, 125
Charles III, King of England, 1–2
Chiaramonte, Linda, 33
Chronicle of the Horse, The, 11, 19
clothing, riding, 74, 89
Cloud (wild horse), 36, 38
Clydesdales (horse breed), 74
coaching. *See* carriage driving

co-evolution vs domestication, 144
Colby's Crew (rescue group), 103–104
Common Riding. *See* Scotland, riding in
communication skills, 51, 95–96
"Confidante, The" (Kumin), 92
Continental Acres, 72
control, of horses, 23, 25, 99
cosmetics, equine, 88–89
Coss, Brian, 123, 125–126
Cothran, Gus, 37
Cowan, Lyn, 89
Cowgirl Rising (Howell-Sickles), 25
Cowgirls: Women of the American West (Jordan), 25
cruel treatment, of horses
  "big lick" competitions, 96
  in entertainment, 108
  at horse auctions, 108–109
  in literature, 8, 11
  slaughter plant business, 102–105, 108–110
Cumming, Primrose, 92
Custer (wild horse), 35, 37

D

Dampsey, Elizabeth, 56
dangers
  of carriage driving, 77–78
  in endurance riding, 122, 126, 129
  in film, portrayed in, 79–80
  in foxhunting, 44–46
  horse lover's responses to, viii
Daniels, John Sr., 11–12
Dark Horses and Black Beauties: Animals, Women, a Passion (Pierson), 11
Dawson, Phyllis, 134
Day, Emily, 41–42
Day, Jimmy, 42
death, of beloved horses, 16–17, 53–55, 94
Diana, Princess of Wales, 2
dogs, 133, 144. *See also* hounds
domestication vs co-evolution, 144
domestic roles, of women, 15–16
donations, to rescue organizations, 101–102, 104, 111
donkeys, 69, 102–103, 142
driving, carriage. *See* carriage driving
drugs, in race horses, 108
Dunning, Joan, 42

E

economy, role of in horsegirlhood, 92. *See also* finances, of horse lovers
Elizabeth II, Queen of England, 81
empowerment, from horses, 145
endurance riding, 121–130
  about, 122–124
  Cavalry category of, 125
  dangers of, 122, 126, 129
  Federighi and (*see* Federighi, Carol)
  females in, 127–128
  mental endurance of, 127
  Mongol Derby, 121–123, 127, 129–130
  Perkins and, 145
  physical endurance of, 126
  Tevis Cup, 123, 125, 127–128
entertainment, horses in
  books (*see* books, equine)
  film (*see* films, equine)
  television, 10, 108
equestrienne. *See* horsegirls/horsewomen
Equitana USA, 86–87
Ethel (donkey), 69
Europe, carriage driving in, 77
Evans, Nicholas, 81
expos, equine, 86–87

F

Facebook, rescue organizations and, 104–105
family, horses as, 93, 145
fandom, vs horse lovers, 4–5
Farley, Walter, 13
Federighi, Carol
  endurance riding experiences of, 121–122, 125–126, 129
  future riding challenges for, 128–130
  husband and, 123, 125–126
  Mongol Derby and, 121–122, 129–130
female horse riders. *See* horsegirls/horsewomen
feral horses, 35–40, 146
Figure 4 Ranch (NE), 62–63
films, equine, 79–83
  accuracy in, regarding equine use, 82–83
  Black Stallion, The, 13
  documentarian, 39
  Horse Whisperer, The, 79–80
  males as leads in, 81
  National Velvet, 10
finances, of horse lovers, 30, 32–34, 101–102, 104, 111. *See also* economy, role of in horsegirlhood
Foley, Sue, 118
food, horses as, 64–65, 102–104
foxhunting, 41–48
  dangers of, 44–46

fox welfare and, 47
history and, 44
horses for, 41–42
speed in, 46–47
stereotypes in, 41, 43, 46
tradition and, 43
Virginia's landscape as backdrop for, 42, 44, 46–47
Friesians (horse breeds), 73, 82

G
Gabe (Winegar's horse), xiv–xv, 3–4, 16–17, 52–56
Gaucho Derby, 123
Gautier, Jean-Paul, 73
gender equalizer, horses as, 75, 95–96
genetic predispositions, of horse love. *See also* innate, horse love as
bonding with horses and, 146–147
equine attraction and, 142
gender differences, 95–96, 145, 147 (*see also* males)
human-animal bond and, 144, 146
Gilligan, Carol, 95
Gloria (carriage driver)
about, 71–72
accolades of, 77
herd of, 74
as horsegirl, 73, 75
on horsegirlhood, 75–76
Goudge, Elizabeth, 8–9
Greece, ancient, 23

H
Harrison, Jim, 16–17
Hawick (Scotland), 114, 117
Haydon, Cynthia, 76
Haythorn, Craig, 62–63
health-related activities, equine, 88
heartbeats and hoofbeats, 97–98
heart horses, 54–57
heart rate variation (HRV), 56
Henry, Marguerite, 8, 12–13
hoof care, 153
hormone therapy, 87
Horse Angel's Rescue/Sharing and Caring Group (rescue group), 107
horse breeds. *See also* horses
Arabians, 8, 104, 124, 145
Clydesdales, 74
Friesians, 73, 82
Irish draft, 42, 115
Kladrubers, 71, 74
Morabs, 110
Percherons, 23
Standardbreds, 101
Tennessee Walkers, 96
Thoroughbreds, 85, 102, 108–109
horse-drawn vehicles, 74–75. *See also* carriage driving
horsegirls/horsewomen
as book lovers, 9 (*see also* books, equine)
characteristics of, 50–52, 67–68, 135–136 (*see also* innate, horse love as)
class differences of, 3, 25
communication of, with horses, 95–96
cruel treatment of horses by, 96 (*see also* cruel treatment, of horses)
demographics of, ix, 19
on East Coast vs in the West, 25
in endurance riding, 127
fear of perceptions of, 17
growth of, 92
hiding horses from families by (*see* secrets, of horsewomen)
as horses, 87
marital status and motherhood of (*see* marriage; motherhood/mothers)
masculinity of, 76
neurology of attraction/addiction to horses by, 141–143 (*see also* genetic predispositions, of horse love)
recognition of other, 131–133
relationships between (*see* relationships, between horsewomen)
Riding of the Marches, prohibition of in, 114
science and, 55–56 (*see also* genetic predispositions, of horse love)
sexualization of by males (*see* sexualization, of horse riding)
as teenagers, 25–26, 51, 88, 94–95
types of, 68
as wild at heart, 137–140
horse lovers
books and, 7–13 (*see also* books, equine)
carriage driving and, 71–78 (*see also* carriage driving)
characteristics of, 131–136
demographics of, ix, 19
endurance riding and, 121–130 (*see also* endurance riding)
films, 79–83 (*see also* films, equine)
foxhunting and, 41–48 (*see also* foxhunting)

genetic predispositions of, 141–147 (*see also* genetic predispositions, of horse love)
heart horses and, 54–57
horsegirlhood, phenomenon of, 91–100 (*see also* horse lovers as females, suppositions for)
marriage and, 15–19 (*see also* marriage)
rescue organizations and, 101–112 (*see also* rescue organizations, equine)
Scotland, riding in, 113–120 (*see also* Scotland, riding in)
secrets of, 29–34 (*see also* secrets, of horsewomen)
sexualization and, 21–28 (*see also* sexualization, of horse riding)
traits of, 49–52 (*see also* innate, horse love as)
Western Challenge and, 59–70 (*see also* Western Challenge)
as wild at heart, 137–140
wild horse protection and, 35–40
Winegar as, 1–5 (*see also* Winegar, Karin)
worship, horse love as, 85–90
horse lovers as females, suppositions for
aesthetic/beauty and, 96
for bodily freedom, 89, 100
cultural reasons, 95
emotional attachments, 108 (*see also under this heading* relational nature of horses)
for empowerment and value, 145
as gender equalizer, 75, 95–96
for independence/freedom, 70, 75, 89
as innate, 5, 55, 65, 110, 117, 128, 134–135, 146, 154 (*see also* genetic predispositions, of horse love)
judgment, absence of, 26
life's transitions, marking of, 88
nurturing nature of females, 70, 104, 128
for power and control, 25, 51, 75, 89, 138
relational nature of horses, 9, 50–51, 75, 95–96, 145
horse-packing, 128–129
horses
accurate use of in films, 82–83
archetypes of, 143
attractions to as sexual (*see* sexualization, of horse riding)
beauty of, 96
breeds (*see* horse breeds)
cruel treatment of (*see* cruel treatment, of horses)
family, as substitute for, 27, 55
as family, 93, 145
in film, accurate use of, 82–83
as food, 64–65, 102–104
for foxhunting, 41–42
as gender equalizers, 75, 95–96
health of, in endurance riding, 123–124
physiological effect of on humans, 56
power and, 75, 143
relational nature of, 9, 50–52, 75, 95–96, 145
riding, first time, 138
as therapeutic, 48, 50–51, 61
toy, 96
wild, 35–40, 146
Horse Whisperer, The, 79–80
horse whisperer training technique, 81
horseyback rides (human, as play), 25
hounds, 64–65, 68. *See also* dogs; foxhunting
Howell-Sickles, Donna, 25
HRV (heart rate variation), 56
Hunting Wild Horses and Burros on Public Lands Act, 40
husbands, of horsewomen, 123, 125–126. *See also* secrets, of horsewomen

I

In a Different Voice (Gilligan), 95
independence, horses as source of, 70, 75, 89
innate, horse love as, 5, 55, 65, 110, 117, 128, 134–135, 146, 154. *See also* genetic predispositions, of horse love
introverts, 52, 68–69
Ireland, male riders in, 117–118
Irish draft (horse breed), 42, 115

J

James, Will, 12
Johnston, Velma Bronn (Wild Horse Annie), 40
Jordan, Teresa, 25
Josie (Western Challenge horse), 59, 61, 66
Judy (trainer), 22, 50, 54
Jung, Carl, 143
Jurga, Fran, 12

K

Kailzie Equestrian Centre, 115
Kathrens, Ginger, 35–40
Kayne, Susan, 108–110
Kennedy, Jackie, 44

kids, horses' treatment of vs adults, 61
kill buyer pens, 102–103
King of the Wind (Henry), 8, 13
Kingston (Riding the Marches horse), 113, 115–117
Kittelson, Mary Lynn, 99
Kladrubers (horse breed), 71, 74
Kumin, Maxine, 25, 91–93, 96

L

"Lamed Mare, The" (Lewis), 89
Lanata, Antonio, 56
language, for love of an animal, 26, 55
Lawrence, Elizabeth, 27, 88, 93–97
Leck, Anne, 76
legislation, wild horse protection, 40
Lewis, Lisa, 89
library, of equestrian books, 11–12
literature, equine. *See* books, equine; poetry, equine
Little White Horse, The (Goudge), 8–9
Lloyd, Lynn, 59, 64–68
Lucy (foxhunting friend), 42–48, 79–80

M

Mackay-Smith, Alexander, 11, 42
Mackay-Smith, Matthew, 41
magic, horses and, 143
males
  anatomy of as suited for riding, vs females, 118
  animal relationships and, 100, 145
  attention span of, 118
  carriage driving and, 76
  communication skills of, 95–96
  in competitions, 145
  as employees, 68
  in endurance riding, 127
  in equine media, 89
  on females in rodeo culture, 97
  in films, 81
  human-horse relationship, as dismissive of, 94 (*see also under this heading* sexualization, of horse riding by)
  Ireland, riders in, 117–118
  in kill buying businesses, 105–108
  on marriage and horses, 32, 94
  passions, double standard of relinquishing after marriage, 18
  in rescue industry, 106, 108
  as riders, in Scotland, 114
  as riders in Virginia, 46
  secrets kept from, by wives (*see* secrets, of horsewomen)
  sexualization, of horse riding by, 22–24, 26–27 (*see also* sexualization, of horse riding)
  as threatened by horses, 31–33
  as wild horse advocates, 37
marriage. *See also* motherhood/mothers
  horse riding as secrets in (*see* secrets, of horsewomen)
  horses as substitute for, 27, 55
  horses on dynamic of, 95
  males on horses and, 32, 94
  riding, relinquished for, 17–19, 75
  riding, returned to post, 25–26
  shared love of riding in, 123, 125–126
  status, of horsewomen, 19, 51–52, 92
  of Winegar, 16, 18
  women's domestic role in, 15–16
masculinity, of horsewomen, 76
McIntosh, Suzie, 115
McLaughlin, Castle, 12
McWhirter, Barbara, 104
media, 7–8, 89, 108
meditation, 154
men. *See* males
Middleburg (VA), 44, 46
midlife crises, males vs females, 45
Miller, Carol, 134
Misty of Chincoteague (Henry), 12
model horses, 96
Molly (Winegar's pony), viii–ix, xiii–xiv, 143
Mongol Derby, 121–123, 127, 129–130
Morabs (horse breed), 110
Morgan, Collette, 9–10
motherhood/mothers
  childfree by choice, horsewomen as, 19, 51–52, 133
  horses as substitute for, 27, 55
  horses related to archetypes of, 143
  horsewomen's relationships with, 50, 52
riding, relinquished for, 17–19, 31, 51–52, 75
mourning, of beloved horses, 16–17, 53–55, 94
mules, 102–103, 142
music, hoofbeats like, 97–98
Mustangs, 35, 39–40, 146
My Little Pony toys and musical, 143

N

National Sporting Library (NSL), 11–12, 42
National Velvet (Bagnold), 10
natural horsemanship, 81

nature, 67, 97
Nevada landscape, 64

O

ocean gallop, 119
off-the-track Thoroughbreds (OTTBs), 108–109
Ohrstrom, George L. Sr., 11
Old Dominion Hundred, 125
Ott, Kathy, 33–34
Outlander (tv series), 113, 119
"Over the Sea to Skye" (*Outlander* theme song), 119

P

Parker, Penny, 107
passions
  female's entitlement to, 17
  horse rescue and, 106–107
  importance of, 73
  relationships and, 50–51, 55
past lives, 66
Percherons (horse breed), 23
performance drugs, in race horses, 108
Perkins, Anne, 144–147
physiological impact, of horses on humans, 56
Pierson, Melissa Holbrook, 11
pipers, 119
play, horse, 25, 87, 96
PMU (pregnant mare's urine), 87
poetry, equine, 16–17, 89, 91–93
polo, 2
ponies, 77, 103. *See also* Molly (Winegar's pony)
postmenopausal medication, 87
power
  bodily, 89
  from cruel treatment of horses, 96
  horse love as, vs males cravings for, 28
  from horses, 75
  horses as representation of, 143
  lack of in females, 34
  as male perspective of horsewomen, 13, 23
  workplace, and horse similarities, 51
pregnant mare's urine (PMU), 87
Prior-Palmer, Lara, 122
Pryor Mountain Wild Horse Range, 35–39
psyches, horse impact on, 99–100
psychotherapy, human-horse relationships as, 48, 50–51, 61

Q

Quarter Horse ranch (NE), 62–63

R

race horses, drugs given to, 108
Race the Wild Coast (South Africa), 130
ranchers, wild horses and, 38, 40
Rayoff, Terra, 106
Red Rock Ranch (NV), 64
refuges, wild horse, 37–38
reincarnation, 66
relational nature of horses, 9, 50–51, 75, 95–96, 145
relationships, between horsewomen
  childhood, of Winegar, viii–ix
  hospitality of, 64, 76, 87
  recognition of others in public, 131–133
  for rescue of horses, 110
  in riding adventures, with friends, 42–48, 59–63, 66, 70
  in riding adventures, with strangers, 64–65, 114–116, 119–120
  at stables, 88
rescue organizations, equine, 101–112
  about, 101–102
  Arabian Kill Pen and Auction Horse Group/The Arabian 300 Club, 104–105
  call to participate in, by horsewomen, 101–102, 104–106
  Colby's Crew, 103–104
  females in, 102–104, 107–108
  financial aspect of, 101–102, 104, 111
  Horse Angel's Rescue/Sharing and Caring Group, 107
  slaughter plant business, 102–105, 108–111
  Stone Valley's Ray of Hope Equine Rescue, 106
  Unbridled Thoroughbred Foundation, 108–110
  Winegar's experience with, 101–102, 110–112
retail, equine, 4–5, 86, 88–89. *See also* books, equine
rhythms, horse, 97–98
Richards, John, 77
rideouts, in Scotland. *See* Scotland, riding in
riding
  composure of rider, importance of, 65
  dangers of (*see* dangers)
  endurance (*see* endurance riding)
  as escape, 129–130, 153
  foxhunting (*see* foxhunting)

love of, reasons for (*see* horse lovers as females, suppositions for)
male distortion of (*see* sexualization, of horse riding)
males and, 46, 114, 117–118, 127, 145
relinquished for marriage/motherhood, 17–19, 31, 51–52, 75
vacation in Scotland (*see* Scotland, riding in)
in Washington, D.C., 122, 124, 126, 128
in Western Challenge (*see* Western Challenge)
Riding the Marches. *See* Scotland, riding in
rituals, of horse ownership, 153–154
Robin (horse rescuer), 104–105
Robinson, Gay, 76
Rock Creek Stables (D.C.), 123–124, 126
rodeo culture, 97
rodeos, Mexican, 103
Roy, Suzanne, 40
royalty faux pas, 1–2
runaways, carriage driving, 77–78

S

Scanlan, Lawrence, 12
Schapiro, Nancy, 133
Schork, Christopf, 125
science, of horse lovers, 55–56
Scotland, riding in, 113–120
evening activities during, 117, 119
history of, 114
horse of, 113, 115–117
members of ride (human and horse), 114–115
ocean gallop and, 119
Sea Fighter (foxhunting horse), 41
Seaton, Muffy, 27
secrets, of horsewomen, 29–34
accommodations made by veterinarian for, 33–34
divorce and, 32
from shop owner perspective, 30–31, 33
Winegar's experience with, 31
Seven Sets of Horseshoes: An American Journey (Lloyd), 67
sexualization, of horse riding, 21–28
control and, 23, 25
horses as sexual, 23–24
horsewomen's reputation among males and, 22–23, 27–28
Jung on, 143
ogling, Winegar's experience with, 26
stereotype of as embarrassing to young riders, 25–26
virginity and, 28
Shadow (Winegar's horse), 57
Shagyas (Arabian strain), 124
"Silver Snaffles" (Kumin), 92
slaughter business, 102–105, 108–110
Slocum, Edee, 59, 62, 65–66, 70. *See also* Western Challenge
Slocum, Sue, 59–63, 66, 70. *See also* Western Challenge
Smith, Ally, 103–104
Smoky The Cowhorse (James), 12
sound, 97–99
Sounding the Soul: The Art of Listening (Kittelson), 99
Spanish horses, 37
sports, equestrian, 7–8, 42, 95, 118
stables/barns
rituals in, 153–154
Rock Creek Stables (D.C.), 123–124, 126
tour of, Kentucky, 85–86
Winegar's childhood, viii–ix, 134, 139
as worship places, 88
Standardbreds (horse breed), 101
state of coherence, 56
Stone Valley's Ray of Hope Equine Rescue, 106
Suhr, Julie, 24, 127–128

T

teenage riders, 25–26, 51, 88, 94–95
television, horses on, 10, 108, 113, 119
Tennessee Walkers (horse breed), 96
Terry (at Western Challenge), 64–65, 68–69
Tevis Cup, 123, 125, 127–128
therapy, horses as, 48, 50–51, 61
Thoroughbreds (horse breed), 85, 102, 108–109
Title IX, 95
Titus, Dina, 40
trainers, qualities of, 93
transcontinental ride, 67
trots, rhythms of, 97–98
trust building, 51

U

Unbridled (tv series), 108
Unbridled Thoroughbred Foundation (rescue group), 108
unicorns, 99

V

Vanderbilt, Alfred, 77

Vermont Challenge, 126
veterinarians, 33–34
Virginia, foxhunting in, 42, 44, 46–47
virginity, 28, 99–100
von Hünersdorf, Ludwig, 11–12

W

Warner, Melissa, 73
Washington, D.C., riding in, 122, 124, 126, 128
wedding, horses in, 34
Western Challenge, 59–70
  about, 60
  Lynn Lloyd and, 59, 64, 66–68
  ride of, 65–66, 69
  social time and, 64–65
  travel to, 60–64
whip, in carriage driving, 73
"Why is it That Girls Love Horses?" (Kumin), 92
Wild About Horses (Scanlan), 12
Wild Horse and Burro Protection Act, 40
Wild Horse Annie (Velma Bronn Johnston), 40
wild horses, 35–40, 146
Winants, Peter, 46
Winegar, Karin
  barn, childhood, viii–ix, 134, 139
  books, influential to, 8–9, 12–13
  carriage driving and, 21, 23, 72, 97–98
  childhood, horse love during, xiii–xiv, 134, 137–139, 143
  driving runaways and, 77–78
  early years of, 3–4
  father, relationship with, 24–25
  foxhunting experience of, 41–48 (*see also* foxhunting)
  friends of, as not supportive, 116
  friends of, childhood, viii–ix
  Gabe (horse), xiv–xv, 16–17, 53–56
  independence of, 16
  Josie, ridden in Western Challenge, 59–61, 66, 69
  Kingston, ridden in Scotland, 113, 115–117
  marriage of, 16, 18
  Molly (pony), viii–ix, xiii–xiv, 143
  ogling, experience with, 26
  rescue organizations, experience with, 101–102, 110–111
  riding, Shadow vs Smokey, 149–152
  Scotland, riding vacation in (*see* Scotland, riding in)
  Sea Fighter, ridden during foxhunting, 41, 45–47
  Shadow (horse), 57
  Stetson and Bakari, ridden in D.C., 124, 126, 128
  Washington, D.C., riding in, 122, 124, 126, 128
  Western Challenge and (*see* Western Challenge)
  wild horse protection range experience and, 35–39
wolves, 139–140
women. *See* horsegirls/horsewomen
"Women and Horses" (Kumin), 93
Woolley, Pamela, 135–136
World Coaching Club, The, 76
worship, horse love as, 86–88, 92

Shadow and Karin around 2000

About the Author

Karin Winegar writes in-depth biographies, newspaper and magazine features and commentaries. Her work has appeared in the *New York Times*, *Los Angeles Times* and *The Wall Street Journal* as well as publications devoted to sailing, horses, travel, gender equity, ecology, etc. She has won Lowell Thomas Awards for investigative journalism and maritime writing. Her non-fiction book *SAVED: Rescued Animals and The Lives They Transform* features a foreword by Dr. Jane Goodall, prologue by Dr. Temple Grandin and photography by Judy Olausen. Winegar is based in St. Paul, Minnesota where she is founder of Horse Feed Press publishing and custom books.

Horse Feed Press

Horse Feed Press provides custom writing, editing, design, printing and marketing services to those with a story to tell, a history to preserve or a joy to share. It is based in Saint Paul, Minnesota. www.horsefeedpress.com

It takes its name from the fact that any profits go to the author's horse feed bill. The price of *Horse Lovers* is approximately the cost of a bag of Equine Senior, which I donate daily to equine rescue groups.

About This Cover

In spring 2024, I strolled the aisles of the main barn at the annual Horse Expo at the Minnesota State Fairgrounds. Horses, mules, donkeys and ponies of various breeds, sizes and ages from 18 hand Shires to 12 hand Shetlands were enjoying—or just tolerating—the adoring crowds.

A gray Arabian caught my eye, and I moved to his stall door. I had caught his eye, too, perhaps. I scratched his neck, shoulder and throat and rubbed his ears, and he responded with blissful lip twitches and a lowered head. I stayed. And stayed. And came back twice more during the day to cuddle "Monty." Finally, I noticed the pedigree posted on his stall card, and there it was—a common ancestor or three with both Gabe and Shadow, my own Arabians.

A friend snapped a cellphone photo. This cell phone photo. Another friend, a nationally-known photographer, urged me to switch it to black and white, tweaked my face and cropped it. My book designer buffed it (well, me). A handful of friends enthusiastically urged me to use it.

I love my first cover by award-winning artist Donna Howell Sickles, a premier American artist whose work celebrates the joy and mystery of the female attraction to horses.

But I must confess that while I will get on just about any strange horse, adjust my stirrups and ride off, I have much less confidence about being photographed and that photo seen in public. Here it is anyway, because I believe it expresses the love, the empathy that I am seeking to understand—the female love of horses.

By the time a second printing of *Horse Lovers* was needed, I had gathered the self-esteem to use this personal image, which caught me in the tender trance of horse love with Monty. Isn't he fine!